BORROWED LIGHT

BORROWED
LIGHT

Hymn Texts, Prayers and Poems

Thomas H. Troeger

New York   Oxford
OXFORD UNIVERSITY PRESS
1994

Oxford University Press

Oxford   New York   Toronto
Delhi   Bombay   Calcutta   Madras   Karachi
Kuala Lumpur   Singapore   Hong Kong   Tokyo
Nairobi   Dar es Salaam   Cape Town
Melbourne   Auckland   Madrid

and associated companies in
Berlin   Ibadan

Published by Oxford University Press, Inc.
200 Madison Avenue, New York, New York 10016

Oxford is a registered trademark of Oxford University Press

Library of Congress Cataloging-in-Publication Data
Troeger, Thomas H., 1945–
Borrowed light : hymn texts, prayers, and poems /
Thomas H. Troeger.
p.   cm.   Includes indexes.
ISBN 0-19-385942-4 (alk. paper)
1. Hymns, English.   2. Prayer.
3. Christian poetry.
I. Title.
BV459.T76   1994   264′.2—dc20   93-47549

4 6 8 9 7 5

Printed in the United States of America

For M. M.

Unbidden came God's love,
not rushing from the skies
as angel, flame or dove
but shining through your eyes.

Preface

This book gathers together my complete hymn texts, which I have interspersed with related prayers and poems. The prayers deepen and extend the meaning of what the congregation sings. The poems encourage reflection upon the hymns and often reveal a line or an idea that inspired a hymn.

I have grouped the hymns by images and patterns of association. This allows the reader to trace the web of metaphor and meaning that pervades the collection.

There are endnotes and indexes according to meter, theme and image, Scripture, and first lines, to help pastors, church musicians, liturgists, and composers locate precisely what they need. However, one of the most productive ways to use the book in preparing for worship is to read a number of texts in sequence, allowing the flow of images to awaken prayer and engage the imagination. The Afterword provides further material for this creative process by exploring the literary and theological understandings that shape my hymnody.

May borrowed light shine through these pages as a witness

to Christ the pure and primal light
that lightens everyone.

Denver, Colorado   T. H. T.
Summer 1993

Acknowledgments

I am grateful to many congregations, denominational groups, and members of the Hymn Society in the United States and Canada and the Academy of Homiletics, who have encouraged the collecting of these hymns, prayers and poems.   I owe a special debt to the following individuals: Carol Doran, the composer and colleague who first inspired my efforts; John Kuzma, a composer and friend, who has affirmed my early work while leading me in new directions; Jane Smith, the dean of Iliff School of Theology, who has provided strong support for my writing; Sandy Smith, my colleague, who has assisted with her skill at running computers and setting things in order; Laurie Tomlinson, my student assistant, who helped collect and retype early texts; George Black, who served as an editorial consultant for this volume and whose literary analysis of many of my hymn texts has given me new insights about the poetics of hymnody;   Richard French, who read the entire collection and made helpful suggestions about theological and aesthetic concerns; Susan Brailove, who has been instrumental in seeing my work to publication; and Merle Marie, my wife, to whom this book is dedicated in gratitude for her reliable critical judgments and unwavering support.

Contents

Melody Alone

A Spendthrift Lover

A Single Unmatched Stone

Fragmentary Prayers

Disturbance of the Solid Ground

BORROWED LIGHT

1. The Moon with Borrowed Light

The moon with borrowed light
gives witness to the sun,
discreetly fading with the night
when morning has begun.
John's borrowed light was drawn
from heaven's vibrant rays,
his life a witness to the dawn
of Christ's approaching blaze.

When temple Levites asked
what title did John claim,
he said he had a single task
a single goal and aim:
to redirect their sight
beyond what he had done
to Christ the pure and primal light
that lightens everyone.

The clouds of sin yet mask
earth's tangled, stubbly ground,
and O how many hearts still ask
where God's clear path is found.
For borrowed light we pray
so we may be a sign
that points to Christ, the truth, the way,
the life, the light divine.

2. Swiftly Pass the Clouds of Glory

Swiftly pass the clouds of glory,
heaven's voice, the dazzling light;
Moses and Elijah vanish—
Christ alone commands the height!
Peter, James and John fall silent,
turning from the summit's rise
downward toward the shadowed valley
where their Lord has fixed his eyes.

Glimpsed and gone the revelation—
they shall gain and keep its truth
not by building on the mountain
any shrine or sacred booth
but by following the savior
through the valley to the cross
and by testing faith's resilience
through betrayal, pain and loss.

Lord, transfigure our perception
with the purest light that shines
and recast our life's intentions
to the shape of your designs
till we seek no other glory
than what lies past Calvary's hill
and our living and our dying
and our rising by your will.

3. Density of Light

Density of light
that could shatter the cold rock of the moon,
compacted flame
that only the face of holy love could withstand,
may Christ reflect your blaze
to the distant satellite of my heart
and melt the fear
that from the orbit of my days
you would scatter
my dim shards to darkness.

Sudden lightning
in the middle of night,
showing me
a vast land and a twisting trail
are waiting
where all I have seen is a wall of darkness,
persist in me as hope
and as strength to finish my descent
from the mountain through the valley
toward an open field I cannot see.

Density of light,
compacted flame,
sudden lightning,
draw me onward through thick darkness
trusting
that light shall spring from the grave
and the coldest rock in space
shall join in a blaze of song:
glory, glory, glory
glory be to you O God.

4.   Let the Truth Shine in Our Speaking

Let the truth shine in our speaking
as the sun in fields by day,
as the pure and slantless streaming
of the noon's revealing ray
washing earth in heaven's brightness
with the light from straight above,
then we shall be faithful neighbors
linked by Christ's deceitless love.

When we wound or grieve each other
let us name the wrong that's done
but not bear our hurt and anger
past the setting of the sun.
For the sin of keeping silent,
is the storm that never comes
or that afterward still lingers
sounding yet its grumbling drums.

As the vesperal light is falling
and the air is cooling down,
as we smell the pines and cedars
and the breathings of the ground,
let Christ's richer, mystic fragrance
rise from hearts this day redeemed
when we spoke the truth as neighbors
while the sunlight brightly streamed.

5. Listen to the Cloud that Brightens

Listen to the cloud that brightens
hearts that stumble in the shade.
Hear the cloud of great believers,
heed the witness they have made:
prophets who have raged in judgment,
martyrs killed by flame and sword,
bold reformers through the ages,
common folk who loved the Lord.

Their distinctly human features
have been smoothed by years of praise
and the mystic sacred aura
that encircles ancient days,
yet those sainted holy figures
once like us were blood and bone,
troubled by the same temptations,
doubts and questions we have known.

Here they made their costly witness,
here upon this trodden ground
where the one whose path they followed
with a wreath of thorns was crowned.
Now they call from that dominion
past the range of mortal sight,
joined with Christ in one communion
of eternal song and light.

As a crowd's impassioned cheering
fuels a runner's flagging pace
so the cloud's enraptured singing
strengthens us to run our race.
We can hear them in our worship,
we can sense them through our prayers,
we can see their witness living
in their brave and faithful heirs.

All who pray and act for justice,
all whose love pours out in deeds,
all who waken social systems
to the cry of human needs,
all who bear their neighbor's burden,
all who lift the soul that faints—
all of these on earth together
sing with heaven's cloud of saints:

"Lay aside whatever holds you
from the gospel's shining goal,
any sin or weight that's dragging
at your heart or mind or soul.
Fix your mind alone on Jesus,
who endured the cross and shame,
and press on with perseverance
for the glory of his name!"

6. Writing at Dusk

When day is letting go,
the mind may follow too
and what we could not find by light
the dark may bring to view.
The words that would not come,
the phrases never found,
present themselves at night:
perfect, obvious
right in sense and sound.

7. Direct Us, Lord, through Darkness

Direct us, Lord, through darkness
to gain that keener sight
which draws the heart to ponder
the farthest, faintest light—
the stars beyond our reaching
that share the dust you formed
to make us earthen creatures
you breathed upon and warmed.

From your configuration
of elemental dust
arise our need and yearning
to reach toward you in trust—
to live by faith that widens
the wonder in the mind
that breath and flesh and planets
and stars are intertwined!

The bonds of primal matter
that link the earth and sky
are deepened and extended
by faith's alerted eye
which scans the stars recalling
the one through whom we pray
was born as dust in darkness
and is our light and way.

Hidden Water

8. The Hidden Stream that Feeds

The hidden stream that feeds
our daily acts of care
springs forth in worship when Christ leads
the church in song and prayer.

Lord, through our lives may others hear
your living waters drawing near.

The stream runs clear and deep
and tastes of heaven's skies
and where its ceaseless currents sweep
flows life that never dies.

Lord, through our lives may others hear
your living waters drawing near.

A heart of stone and dust,
of withered hopes and dreams,
becomes a spring of faith and trust
by drinking from these streams.

Lord, through our lives may others hear
your living waters drawing near.

We leave this watered place
to work on rocky ground
yet even there the streams of grace
sustain our daily round.

Lord, through our lives may others hear
your living waters drawing near.

9.   Water Moving though Stone

Water moving through stone,
fire in zero cold,
wind dispersing heavy air:
     flow,
     burn,
     blow—
awaken prayer:
come and enfold
my heart as your own.

10. The First Day of Creation

The first day of creation
is dawning in the soul,
upon the deep God hovers
where fear and chaos roll.
The inward dark is parting.
The seas make room for land.
Great shorelines are emerging,
a new world is at hand!

Yet God is recreating
more than our inner world:
look up beyond the planets
where galaxies are swirled,
look out and see how often
surprising love is shown.
Christ is at work reshaping
both stars and hearts of stone.

All life in Christ is compassed
by the transforming grace
that spins new worlds and wonders
in every time and place.
O Twirler of the stardust,
O Light no darkness rims,
your new creation pulses
with worship, praise and hymns.

11. God Marked a Line and Told the Sea

God marked a line and told the sea
its surging tides and waves were free
to travel up the sloping strand
but not to overtake the land.

God set one limit in the glade
where tempting, fruited branches swayed,
and that first limit stands behind
the limits that the law defined.

The line, the limit and the law
are patterns meant to help us draw
a bound between what life requires
and all the things our heart desires.

But discontent with finite powers,
we reach to take what is not ours
and then defend our claim by force
and swerve from life's intended course.

We are not free when we're confined
to every wish that sweeps the mind
but free when freely we accept
the sacred bounds that must be kept.

12. A New Line of Shore

It used to be that the island of sand,
where the sea grass grows and the sea gulls land,
was moored by a thin line of beach to the shore.
We often walked out there, some half mile or more,
pretending when we stood on the tip
we commanded the prow of a private ship
and had tossed off our lines and were underway,
you and I alone, sailing out from the bay.

Despite the loss of the land to the sea
the waves have not changed the shoreline in me.
Fixed in my mind is the shape of that beach
and the point we used to be able to reach,
but drawn off like sand in the undertow
are things we said we would never let go.
Seashore promises I now reckon them all,
though I thought they'd resist as a bouldered wall
the lick of the tide and the lunge of the storm.

I notice today that the breakers form
from island to shore in a straight white line
as the swells rub against the strand's buried spine,
which lies in the shallows, not in the deep,
like the memory of vows we failed to keep.
Sometimes the current will bring back the sand
and the waves toss up a new rise of land.
Sometimes the heart will lift our vows from its floor
and the inward sea shapes a new line of shore.

13.   The Lick of the Tide, the Lunge of the Storm

The lick of the tide, the lunge of the storm
are shifting the beach and changing its form.
The rivers and rains are resculpting the hill—
but nothing's eroding the Lord's loving will.

The tree from the seed is slowly unfurled,
then felled at its height when lightning is hurled.
The towering wood lies in ash on the earth,
but flame has not damaged the source of rebirth.

The child in our arms we cradle and hold
is one day grown up and one day grown old.
Each muscle and bone knows the forces and strain
that level high mountains to valley and plain.

Resilient with power, one truth shall not bend
to tide or to storm, to lightning or wind:
the love of our God that we breathe with each breath
is with us forever in life and in death.

14. The Sails Were Spilling Wind

The sails were spilling wind,
the boat was taking waves.
The mast began to bend.
Then called the Lord who saves:

"Be still, be still, and rage no more!
Let peace descend on sea and shore."

The sea became a glass,
reflecting heaven's light.
The storm completely passed
when Jesus said that night:

"Be still, be still, and rage no more!
Let peace descend on sea and shore."

Then heading toward the land,
they marveled on the way
that Jesus could command
and make the sea obey:

"Be still, be still, and rage no more!
Let peace descend on sea and shore."

The storm returns again.
In every heart it raves
until we hear again
the Lord who told the waves:

"Be still, be still, and rage no more!
Let peace descend on sea and shore."

This warring world shall end
unless we make it clear
the One who tamed the wind
can tame our hate and fear:

"Be still, be still, and rage no more!
Let peace descend on sea and shore."

Through every act and word
of all our living days
may Christ's own voice be heard
until the world obeys:

"Be still, be still, and rage no more!
Let peace descend on sea and shore."

15.   On the Sand, in the Sun

On the sand, in the sun
where the waters break and run
I have fixed my heart and eye
at the edge of sea and sky
while the breakers like a drum
say he will, he will not come.

What is true I can't decide:
it depends on wind and tide.

While I bear the heat of noon
I am dreaming of the moon
and the evening calm and cool
and the bay a wading pool
where the ripples lap the sand
while I feel his breath and hand.

What is true I can't decide:
it depends on wind and tide.

When the heat grows more intense
I confuse my hope and sense
that far out beyond the shore
where the seagulls dip and soar
each splash of sea appears
a schooner's wake that nears.

What is true I can't decide:
it depends on wind and tide.

As the sea and sky unite
at the fading of the light
and the darkness overcomes
what the daylight ocean drums
I catch a sail against the stars—
or the glint of shoals and bars.

What is true I can't decide:
it depends on wind and tide.

In the darkness let me sleep,
there's no need for me to keep
the watch that's never brought
what my eyes and heart have sought.
A homeward gale in dreams will blow
or will I hear the undertow?

What is true I can't decide:
it depends on wind and tide.

16. Praise to the Spinner Who Twisted and Twirled

Praise to the spinner who twisted and twirled
from seafoam and sunlight the life of this world.
Those same nimble fingers have gathered and fed
my joys and my sorrows into faith's single thread.

Praise to the weaver whose mystical loom
wove order and light from the chaos and gloom.
The shuttle that textured the night with the day
has woven together twines of grace with my clay.

Praise to the tailor whose needle has cast
the stitches of hope that have held my heart fast
and bound as one fabric without any seams
my highest, best visions with Spirit's deep dreams.

Spinner and Weaver and Tailor of all,
this day I acknowledge your wonderful call,
and I ask through the sacraments, worship and prayer
my life will make plain, Lord, it's your vestments I wear.

17.   Who Commands Vast Worlds in Motion?

1. *Solo:*   Who commands vast worlds in motion?
   All: Who commands vast worlds in motion?
   S.   God rules all:
   A.   Heaven and earth and ocean,
         Heaven and earth and ocean.

2. Solo: Planets, moons and stars—God made
         them,
   All: Planets, moons and stars—God made
         them.
   S.   God made them!
   A.   God who with light arrayed them,
         God who with light arrayed them.

3. *Solo:*   All God made is in God's keeping,
   All: All God made is in God's keeping.
   S.   So praise God,
   A.   Dancing with joy and leaping,
         Dancing with joy and leaping.

4. *Solo:*   Greet the son whom heaven gave us,
   All: Greet the son whom heaven gave us.
   S.   Christ Jesus!
   A.   Christ who has come to save us,
         Christ who has come to save us.

5. *Solo:*   Crooked lives the Lord will straighten,
   All: Crooked lives the Lord will straighten.
   S.   Christ triumphs
   A.   Over the strength of Satan,
         Over the strength of Satan.

6. *Solo:*   Covenant and law completed,
   All: Covenant and law completed—
   S.   By Christ filled!

A.	Evil and death defeated,	
	Evil and death defeated.	

7. | *Solo:* | Praise the one whose hand unchains you,
   | *All:* | Praise the one whose hand unchains you,
   | *S.* | All people.
   | *A.* | Jesus, whose love sustains you,
   | | Jesus, whose love sustains you.

8. | *Solo:* | Citizens of every nation,
   | *All:* | Citizens of every nation,
   | *S.* | Give Christ praise,
   | *A.* | Honor and adoration,
   | | Honor and adoration.

9. | *Solo:* | Praise for this eternal treasure,
   | *All:* | Praise for this eternal treasure:
   | *S.* | The Lord's love,
   | *A.* | Greater than human measure,
   | | Greater than human measure.

10. | *Solo:* | Human spirits, tossing, turning,
    | *All:* | Human spirits, tossing, turning
    | *S.* | Need Jesus.
    | *A.* | Jesus will soothe their yearning,
    | | Jesus will soothe their yearning.

11. | *Solo:* | Now my spirit find your center,
    | *All:* | Now my spirit find your center,
    | *S.* | In Jesus.
    | *A.* | Ask for the Lord to enter.
    | | Ask for the Lord to enter.

12. | *Solo:* | Lift to God your heart's thanksgiving,
    | *All:* | Lift to God your heart's thanksgiving
    | *S.* | For Jesus
    | *A.* | And for the Spirit living,
    | | And for the Spirit living.

18. Source and Sovereign, Rock and Cloud

Source and Sovereign, Rock and Cloud,
Fortress, Fountain, Shelter, Light,
Judge, Defender, Mercy, Might,
Life whose life all life endowed:

May the church at prayer recall
that no single, holy name
but the truth that feeds them all
is the God whom we proclaim.

Word and Wisdom, Root and Vine,
Shepherd, Savior, Servant, Lamb,
Well and Water, Bread and Wine,
Way who leads us to I AM:

May the church at prayer recall
that no single, holy name
but the truth that feeds them all
is the God whom we proclaim.

Storm and Stillness, Breath and Dove,
Thunder, Tempest, Whirlwind, Fire,
Comfort, Counselor, Presence, Love,
Energies that never tire:

May the church at prayer recall
that no single, holy name
but the truth that feeds them all
is the God whom we proclaim.

19. Source and Sovereign of All Creation

Source and Sovereign of all creation,
Savior who died and rose and pleads our cause,
Spirit who prays for us in sighs too deep for words,
fix in our hearts
this one unshakable conviction:

Nothing can separate us from your love
in Christ Jesus our Lord.

When those we love suffer and die
and the ground of solid meaning folds beneath our feet
then lead us to stand upon this claim:

Nothing can separate us from your love
in Christ Jesus our Lord.

When we wander in doubt
and our life's purpose fades from view,
steady our wobbling steps with this assurance:

Nothing can separate us from your love
in Christ Jesus our Lord.

When the conflicts and struggles
of the church drive us to our limits,
then renew our common affirmation:

Nothing can separate us from your love
in Christ Jesus our Lord.

When we confront injustice and oppression
and the world rejects our ministry,
strengthen our resolve with this bold truth:

Nothing can separate us from your love
in Christ Jesus our Lord.

Thus strengthened through our daily life
with our last breath we'll say:

Nothing can separate us from your love
in Christ Jesus our Lord.

20. The Sheep Stood Stunned in Sudden Light

The sheep stood stunned in sudden light.
The shepherds shared the creatures' fright,
while heaven's star embroidered train
swept over hills and down the plain.

They heard a rhythmic, rumbling roar,
like breakers breaking on the shore
and running up the thirsty strand
to toss a treasure on the land.

And then the waves began to sing!
A sea of angels, wing on wing,
was circling, chanting in the skies
the news of Christ before their eyes.

This night, O God, again we hear
your hidden ocean drawing near,
again we sense through Jesus' birth
the sea of grace that circles earth.

O when the voiceless night returns
and heaven's sea more softly churns,
may faith be like the shell that sends
the sound of ocean waves and winds.

Through faith we'll hear the angels' song,
and though the dark be deep and long,
we'll bravely live, for by our side
is Christ who came on heaven's tide

21. Wild the Man and Wild the Place

Wild the man and wild the place,
wild his dress and wild his face,
wilder still his words that trace
paths that lead from sin to grace.

"Knock down every proud backed hill!
Every canyon, valley fill!
Plane the soul and pray until
all its raucous rumblings still.

"Throw yourself in Jordan's streams.
Plunge beneath the wave that gleams.
Wash away what only seems.
Rise and float on heaven's dreams.

"Leave on shore unneeded weight,
fear and doubt, the skeptic's freight.
Toss them off and do not wait.
Time is short. The hour is late.

"One now comes whose very name
makes my words seem mild and tame.
I use water to reclaim
lives that he will cleanse with flame.

"You will see him soon appear:
One whose steps through prayer you hear.
Christ is drawing, drawing near,
Christ is coming, coming here!"

22.   What King Would Wade through Murky Streams

What king would wade through murky streams
and bow beneath the wave,
ignoring how the world esteems
the powerful and brave?

Water, River, Spirit, Grace,
sweep over me, sweep over me—
recarve the depths your fingers traced
in sculpting me.

Christ gleams with water brown with clay
from land the prophets trod.
Above him while the clouds give way
descends the dove of God.

Water, River, Spirit, Grace,
sweep over me, sweep over me—
recarve the depths your fingers traced
in sculpting me.

Come bow with Christ beneath the wave.
He stands here at your side
and raises you as from the grave
God raised him crucified.

Water, River, Spirit, Grace,
sweep over me, sweep over me—
recarve the depths your fingers traced
in sculpting me.

23.   O Praise the Gracious Power

O praise the gracious power
that tumbles walls of fear
and gathers in one house of faith
all strangers far and near:

We praise you Christ!
Your cross has made us one!

O praise persistent truth
that opens fisted minds
and eases from their anxious clutch
the prejudice that binds:

We praise you Christ!
Your cross has made us one!

O praise inclusive love
encircling every race,
oblivious to gender, wealth,
to social rank or place:

We praise you Christ!
Your cross has made us one!

O praise the word of faith
that claims us as God's own,
a living temple built on Christ,
our rock and corner stone:

We praise you Christ!
Your cross has made us one!

O praise the tide of grace
that laps at every shore
with visions of a world at peace
no longer bled by war:

We praise you Christ!
Your cross has made us one!

O praise the power, the truth,
the love, the word, the tide.
Yet more than these, O praise their source,
praise Christ the crucified:

We praise you Christ!
Your cross has made us one!

O praise the living Christ
with faith's bright songful voice!
Announce the gospel to the world
and with these words rejoice:

We praise you Christ!
Your cross has made us one!

24.   O Gracious Power

O Gracious Power,
You made us in your image
to be one human family
gathered in one house of faith
with one spirit of peace and joy.

But we have ignored your intention.
We have built a wall between the nations,
a wall between women and men,
a wall between the rich and poor,
a wall between the strong and weak,
a wall between the races,
a wall between people like us
and those who are different.

Give us a vision of your inclusive love,
that by the ministries of music and word,
sacrament and service
we may dismantle the walls of division
and live as one family in the household of faith.

25. Praise the Source of Faith and Learning

Praise the source of faith and learning
who has sparked and stoked the mind
with a passion for discerning
how the world has been designed.
Let the sense of wonder flowing
from the wonders we survey
keep our faith forever growing
and renew our need to pray:

God of wisdom, we acknowledge
that our science and our art
and the breadth of human knowledge
only partial truth impart.
Far beyond our calculation
lies a depth we cannot sound
where your purpose for creation
and the pulse of life are found.

May our faith redeem the blunder
of believing that our thought
has displaced the grounds for wonder
which the ancient prophets taught.
May our learning curb the error
which unthinking faith can breed
lest we justify some terror
with an antiquated creed.

As two currents in a river
fight each other's undertow
till converging they deliver
one coherent steady flow,
blend, O God, our faith and learning
till they carve a single course
while they join as one returning
praise and thanks to you their source.

Wind and Flame

26. First the Wind upon the Water

First the wind upon the water
as the formless sea is stirred,
then the source and core of being
speaks the potent primal word:

Let there be light, let there be sky,
let there be land and living things,
each according to its kind
having fins or hoofs or wings.
Let the complemental images
of men and women shine
with that whole and perfect likeness
of the one who is divine.

First the gathering of matter
in explosive densities
whose compacted masses scatter
through the vast immensities:

Then waves of light that strike the earth
and rains and winds and thunderstorms
turn the dust we share with stars
to a host of living forms.
Thus the generating processes
of atoms, suns and cells
waken that same sense of wonder
that the ancient Scripture tells.

First the wind upon the water,
first the starry cosmic flame,
then the word of the creator
working in the human frame:

Let there be love, let there be grace,
let health and peace and justice rise,
let your science feed your faith
and your knowledge make you wise.

Center all your aims and purposes
in what this world displays:
that the source and core of being
calls for everlasting praise.

27. The Bush in Flame but Not Consumed

The bush in flame but not consumed
that blazed on Horeb's height
confounds the truth we once assumed
by our own shadowed light
reminding us how much we owe
to those who made their aim
refining what faith seeks to know
in fierce but kindly flame.

> Ignite in us, O holy blaze,
> the faith our founders knew.
> By lives that test the roots of praise
> we serve and honor you.

We trace through deep and tangled wood
the unexpected turns
that lead us onward toward this good
for which creation yearns:
disclosure that all life is more
than human thought can frame—
there breathes a mystery at the core,
I Am, I Am by name.

> Ignite in us . . .

I Am, I Am provokes our hearts
to deeper thought and prayer
and brings a vision that imparts
the faith to hope and dare
that through our deeds God will be blessed,
God's word will clearly sound
and by our lives we will attest
we stand on holy ground.

> Ignite in us . . .

But where we stand we cannot stay
because the fiery light
is moving on to mark the way
through wilderness and night,
to bring us through the seas of fear
and draw us on to claim
the visions we have seen appear
in fierce but kindly flame.

> Ignite in us . . .

28. Though Every Sun Shall Spend Its Fire

Though every sun shall spend its fire
and galaxies shall dim to shade,
the Light by whom these lights were made
shall never flicker, never fade.

The Light of lights that danced and played
in Simeon's rejoicing face
shone through each word the old man prayed
to realms beyond the temple's space.

"Your servant, Lord, let now depart.
I've seen the Christ. In peace I go.
What shines in heaven shines below,
your light to every land you show."

In us arise, O Light of lights.
Burn brightly in the caverned heart.
Consume the shade that fear supplies,
and peace and truth instead impart.

29.   Wind Who Makes All Winds that Blow

Wind who makes all winds that blow—
gusts that bend the saplings low,
gales that heave the sea in waves,
stirrings in the mind's deep caves—
aim your breath with steady power
on your church, this day, this hour.
Raise, renew the life we've lost,
Spirit God of Pentecost.

Fire who fuels all fires that burn—
suns around which planets turn,
beacons marking reefs and shoals,
shining truth to guide our souls—
come to us as once you came:
burst in tongues of sacred flame!
Light and Power, Might and Strength,
fill your church, its breadth and length.

Holy Spirit, Wind and Flame,
move within our mortal frame.
Make our hearts an altar pyre.
Kindle them with your own fire.
Breathe and blow upon that blaze
till our lives, our deeds and ways
speak that tongue which every land
by your grace shall understand.

30. As Trees that Withstand the Wind's Shaking

As trees that withstand the wind's shaking,
their roots grown too deep to be loosened,
plant us deep, O God, in your way, truth and life.

   Alleluia, alleluia!
   Alleluia, alleluia!

As trees that bear fruit in due season,
supplying a feast for your creatures,
let our faith bear fruit in our prayer, work and play.

   Alleluia, alleluia!
   Alleluia, alleluia!

As trees that are planted by water
that nurtures the highest green branches
let us draw, O God, from your pure flowing streams.

   Alleluia, alleluia!
   Alleluia, alleluia!

As trees that shall bloom in the desert
refreshing the land that is barren,
let your love take root where there's doubt, fear and
grief.

   Alleluia, alleluia!
   Alleluia, alleluia!

As trees give us coolness in summer
and soften the blast of the winter,
be our shade and shield from the sun, rain and storm.

   Alleluia, alleluia!
   Alleluia, alleluia!

As trees in a gale give their witness,
your Spirit is not ours to master,
let us move and dance to your wind, will and power.

Alleluia, alleluia!
Alleluia, alleluia!

As trees may be grafted with branches,
implant us by faith in your Spirit,
make us one with you and your son Jesus Christ.

Alleluia, alleluia!
Alleluia, alleluia!

31.   A Single Leaf

A single leaf in late November
tumbled through the air
when all the other leaves were gone
and all the branches bare
and landing in the hemlock bush
on needled boughs of green
it drew my eye to map its shape
as if I had not seen

a single leaf through all the days
I raked and bagged for hours,
then raked and bagged and raked and bagged
while more swept down in showers.

But framed against the evergreen
the palm like, fingered form
reminded me of all the rest
that fell to gale and storm

till in that single blood red leaf
fallen down alone
I traced the shapes I had ignored
that violent winds had blown.

32.   We Travel toward a Land Unknown

We travel toward a land unknown—
God's word our only chart—
and breathe in the wind that has swept and blown
from that land to the human heart,
and on the wind we hear the sound
of Miriam's dance by the sea,
and we dance with the slaves whom Pharaoh bound
but the Lord of hosts set free.

Then where our freedom first was won
we settle down to stay,
but find that the journey has just begun,
that the wind blows another way.
And on the wind we hear the song
of Moses and David and Ruth,
who are giving us strength to right the wrong
and to speak and do the truth.

And when we think the journey's end
is very near at hand
we learn that the road has another bend
and we're far from the promised land,
but then the wind returns and lifts
our heart and our strength and our soul,
and we're filled with the steadfast Christlike gifts
that reveal again our goal:

We travel toward a land unknown,
but all along the route
we're thanking our Lord for the wonders shown
and the faith that has conquered doubt.
Give thanks the wind is blowing still,
and pray that the church may be blessed
with the vision and grace and strength of will
to be faithful on its quest.

33. Go Forth with the Blessing of God

Go forth with the blessing of God
who called Sarah and Abraham
to leave home
for a land they did not know.
Travel with them
believing
in the assurance of God's presence
in unfamiliar places.

Go forth with the blessing of God,
whose liberation of the Hebrews
stirred Miriam to sing and dance.
Celebrate with her
in song and praise
God's liberating power.

Go forth with the blessing of God,
who raised up prophets
to call for justice
and to renew the earth.
Stand firm with them
for what is good and true and right.

Go forth with the blessing of God,
whose word became flesh
and dwelt among us
full of grace and truth.
Embody with Christ the gifts
of healing, feeding, forgiving, renewing.

Go forth with the blessing of God,
who raised Christ from the dead.
Be raised with him
as a sign
that life is stronger than death.

Go forth with the blessing of God,
who empowered the church
with wind and fire.
Be filled with the Spirit
that your life may shine
with the flame of holy love.

Go forth with the blessing of God,
sustained by the vision
of that great day
when all people
with all the elements of the universe
will sing in a multitude of voices:

Praise and glory,
thanksgiving and honour,
power and might
be to our God forever.

34.   Why Stare at Heaven's Distant Blue

"Why stare at heaven's distant blue
when Christ has told you what to do?
Your gaze won't draw the clouds back down
that rose with glory from the ground.
Your Lord now reigns in realms above.
Await God's wind and show God's love."

Deep silence fell upon the air,
and earth seemed lonely, hard and bare,
and where Christ's friends had fixed their eyes
stood only sun and cloud and skies.
Then with a slow reluctant gait
they walked toward home to pray and wait.

That congregation lived between
a well marked past and things unseen.
With Christ no longer at their side,
directly there to teach and guide,
they sought through prayer with one accord
the will of their ascended Lord.

May we be disciplined to face
with that young church's patient grace
the prayerful, seeking, waiting days
that are a part of heaven's ways,
by which we learn how we depend
on God to send the flame and wind.

35. Far Easier to Melt the Gold

Far easier to melt the gold
and smash the brittle clay
of idols that the hand may mold
than change the way we pray.

How tempting for the church to seize
upon familiar forms,
retreating to antiquities
to hide from present storms.

As Judah vainly sought escape
behind the temple walls,
unconsciously, the prayers we shape
may mute the God who calls.

Lord, give your church the grace to bend
from its constricted pose
that we who bear your name may tend
to where your Spirit blows.

Then ancient forms may yet renew
in us their first intent:
to bring and keep us close to you
through prayer and sacrament.

36. God, You Move among Us with Grace

God, you move among us with grace,
with the lift and the sweep
of the wind of the Spirit.

But we often refuse to move with you.
We stiffen our backs
and tighten our souls
and lower our eyes
and mumble that we cannot dance.

Send us the truth that will set us free,
free to bend with your Spirit,
free to follow your beat,
free to give ourselves entirely to you,
free to love and to live
with the grace that is in Christ Jesus our Lord.

37. Suddenly God's Sovereign Wind

Suddenly God's sovereign wind
rushes down from heaven's skies,
love we cannot comprehend
seizes us with great surprise.
Worlds beyond this world of sin
sweep us up: we're born again!

Nicodemus tied and caught
in a web of cautious thought,
in his need to keep control
and protect his privileged role,
could not stretch his mind to see
how rebirth could ever be.

Suddenly God's sovereign wind . . .

Truth that dances past our reach,
like the wind's loose leaf-tongued speech,
often fills us with the fright
Nicodemus felt that night
when his heart and mind were torn
hearing he must be reborn.

Suddenly God's sovereign wind . . .

God release us from our fear.
Christ come close and hold us near.
Wake in us a pure desire
for your kiss, O wind and Fire.
Blow again upon this earth.
Give our trembling flesh rebirth.

Suddenly God's sovereign wind . . .

38.   Eagles' Spiralings Comply

Eagles' spiralings comply
to the densities of sky
and the ceaseless downward tug
of the earth's deep iron core
and what ligaments can bear
tensing flesh and hollow bone
stiff against the rush of air.

Circling, circling,
swooping,
planing,
rising, rising,
heaven gaining!

Lord, you made earth's iron core
and the hollow bone and wind,
and you taught the birds to soar,
showing how their wings must bend
for the mass and speed and force
of the air to lift their weight
as they glide and carve their course—

Circling, circling,
swooping,
planing,
rising, rising,
heaven gaining!

In our muscle and our bone
what the eagle knows is known.
Help the heart now, Lord, to learn
that the freedom it desires,
like all soaring flight, requires
that we bend our strength and skill
to your word and wind and will,

Circling, circling,
swooping,
planing,
rising, rising,
heaven gaining!

Melody Alone

39. The Song and Prayer of Birds

The song and prayer of birds
is melody alone.
Their hymns employ no words.
Their praise is purely tone.

Their song is prayer enough.
Love hears what sound conveys,
and love does not rebuff
a creature's wordless praise.

And so we trust that prayer
does not depend on words
to reach the source of care
who understands the birds.

40. Glory to God Is the Song of the Stars

Glory to God is the song of the stars,
music so deep that the silence is sound,
music too lyric for meter and bars,
flowing as prayer that no language has bound,
gathering out of the reaches of space
measureless praises of infinite grace:

> Glory, glory, glory to God!
>> All of creation
>> sings adoration.
> Glory, glory, glory to God!

Dawn gives the song of the stars to the sun.
Watching its brightness suffusing the skies,
we with the psalmist remember the one
who with compassion and justice supplies
wisdom that shines through commandment and law
waking in us our thanksgiving and awe:

> Glory, glory, glory to God!
>> All of creation
>> sings adoration.
> Glory, glory, glory to God!

Light that's recalling the light in our hearts
falls on the leaves that are feeding the vine,
swells the round fruit with the praise it imparts,
praise we release when we pour out the wine,
singing that Christ is the vine that we share,
branches he feeds through our worship and prayer:

> Glory, glory, glory to God!
>> All of creation
>> sings adoration.
> Glory, glory, glory to God!

Sing with the silence of stars and the sun,
sing by providing for all to be fed,
sing through your actions so justice is done,
sing through your deeds that the gospel may spread
Then when you sing with the sound of your voice,
earth as one chorus will sing and rejoice:

Glory, glory, glory to God!
All of creation
sings adoration.
Glory, glory, glory to God!

41.   With Pipes of Tin and Wood Make Known

With pipes of tin and wood make known
the truth each star displays:
creation is a field that's sown
with seeds of thanks and praise.
Articulate with measured sound
the song that fills all things
for even atoms dance around
and solid matter sings.

With pipes of tin and wood restart
the fire the prophets knew
and fan the flame within the heart
to do what God would do.
Pull out the stops that train the ear—
the strings, the flute and reed—
to listen and more subtly hear
God's call through human need.

With pipes of tin and wood repeat
the music danced and played
to welcome home and warmly greet
the prodigal who strayed.
Let healing harmonies release
the hurts the heart compiles
that God through music may increase
the grace that reconciles.

With pipes of tin and wood disclose
that song the world has blurred,
the hymn of life and love that flows
from God's renewing word.
Then boldly open wide the swell
and with a trumpet call
announce the news we thirst to tell:
that Christ is Lord of all.

42. Make Our Church One Joyful Choir

Make our church one joyful choir
on this glad and festive day
and by song invoke the fire
that invites our hearts to pray:

Shape us, Christ, to live and claim
all it means to bear your name.

Bend us low by song and prayer,
low enough to lift the cross
and to take the weight and bear
love's uncounted final cost.

Shape us, Christ, to live and claim
all it means to bear your name.

Lift us up by song and prayer
till the way we deal with loss
and our acts and words of care
trace the pattern of your cross:

Shape us, Christ, to live and claim
all it means to bear your name.

Bend us, lift us, make us strong,
send us out with wind and fire,
so the world may hear the song
that we offer as your choir:

Shape us, Christ, to live and claim
all it means to bear your name.

43. We Need Each Other's Voice to Sing

We need each other's voice to sing
the song our hearts would raise
to set the whole world echoing
with one great hymn of praise.
We blend our voices to complete
the melody that starts
with God who sets and keeps the beat
that stirs our loving hearts.

We give our alleluias
to the church's common chord:
    Alleluia!
    Alleluia!
Praise, O praise, O praise the Lord!

We need each other's strength to lift
the cross we're called to bear.
Each other's presence is a gift
of God's incarnate care.
When acts of love and tender speech
convey the savior's voice,
our praise exceeds what words can reach
and we with song rejoice:

We give our alleluias
to the church's common chord:
    Alleluia!
    Alleluia!
Praise, O praise, O praise the Lord!

We need each other's views to see
the limits of the mind,
that God in fact turns out to be
far more than we've defined,
that God's one image shines in all,

in every class and race,
and every group receives the call
to sing with faith and grace:
We give our alleluias
to the church's common chord:
    Alleluia!
    Alleluia!
Praise, O praise, O praise the Lord!

We need each other's voice to sing,
each other's strength to love,
each other's views to help us bring
our hearts to God above.
Our lives like coals placed side by side
to feed each other's flame,
shall with the Spirit's breath provide
a blaze of faith to claim:

We give our alleluias
to the church's common chord:
    Alleluia!
    Alleluia!
Praise, O praise, O praise the Lord!

44. Come Singing, Come Singing

Solo: Come singing, come singing:
All: God is love no limit bounds.
S. Set ringing, set ringing
A. All the world with joyful sounds.

S. Blend your adoration
A. With your neighbors' caroling.

S. All in God's creation
A. Have a song of praise to sing.

What the ancient prophets dreamed, now, at last, appears:
God has come to cut a path through our thickest fears.
Joy is rising from a world that's lost, bruised, sad, torn:
Joy because God's son, the savior Christ, is born.

Solo: Come bringing, come bringing
All: Songs of thanks that love abounds.

S. Love's springing, love's springing,
A. Blooming in unlikely grounds.

S. Every race and nation:
A. Sing with joy for all God's done,

S. For your liberation
A. From the tangles you have spun.

What the ancient prophets dreamed, now, at last, appears:
God has come to cut a path through our thickest fears.
Joy is rising from a world that's lost, bruised, sad, torn:
Joy because God's son, the savior Christ, is born.

Solo: Keep singing, keep singing
All: Songs of peace the angels sing.

S. Keep clinging, keep clinging
A. To the hope their anthems bring:

S. Peace shall be the blessing
A. When our daily deeds are one

S. With the heart's confessing
A. And the will of God is done.

What the ancient prophets dreamed, now, at last, appears:
God has come to cut a path through our thickest fears.
Joy is rising from a world that's lost, bruised, sad, torn:
Joy because God's son, the savior Christ, is born.

Solo: Hearts winging, hearts winging
All: At the news that Christ has come,

S. Hope springing, hope springing:
A. Save us, save us, David's son!

S. Join the magi bringing
A. Gifts more golden than the sun.

S. Join creation singing,
A. Praising God's anointed one.

What the ancient prophets dreamed, now, at last, appears:
God has come to cut a path through our thickest fears.
Joy is rising from a world that's lost, bruised, sad, torn:
Joy because God's son, the savior Christ, is born.

45. Pastor, Lead Our Circle Dance

Pastor, lead our circle dance
which the Spirit has begun.
Help us hand in hand advance,
show us how to move as one.
Some demand a driving beat,
others ask to slow the pace.
Teach us how to bend and meet
our conflicted needs with grace.

From the center lead and show
steps and leaps we never tried,
then allow the dance to flow,
dancing with us side by side.
Let each dancer take a turn,
dancing in the center free
so that all can teach and learn
what our circle dance could be.

If the circle gets too tight
stop the dance and don't begin
till our open hands invite
all whom Jesus welcomes in.
For the dance of faith belongs
to the strangers in the street,
and we need their steps and songs
for the dance to be complete.

Pastor, lead our circle dance
as the Spirit leads and calls
till the circle's whole expanse
moves beyond our bounds and walls
and we dance with distant suns
dancing in the dark above,
dancing as creation runs
on the energies of love.

46. Make Your Prayer and Music One

Make your prayer and music one.
Lift your songs of faith as signs
that this world has not undone
heaven's wonderful designs.

Alleluia, alleluia, alleluia
alleluia, alleluia, alleluia,
alleluia!

Thus by hymns at midnight's hour
Paul and Silas, jailed and chained,
witnessed to the savior's power
that shall never be restrained.

Alleluia . . .

Faith their captors thought repressed
rang in song upon the gloom.
Through their music they professed:
Christ is risen from the tomb!

Alleluia . . .

While they filled the dark with song,
earth was shaken by the Lord.
Iron chains were not as strong
as the one their hymns adored.

Alleluia . . .

Sing as Paul and Silas sang.
Let no circling dark or wall
muffle what their praises rang:
Jesus Christ is Lord of all!

Alleluia . . .

47. The Love that Lifted Lyric Praise

The love that lifted lyric praise
from David's harp and shepherd soul
in younger, gladder, golden days
grew deeper as the king grew old.
His sweet, clear voice now cracked and thin,
his hands too stiff to pluck a string,
he still was stirred by faith within
to write one final psalm to sing.

He rummaged through his mind for themes
and stumbled first on early scenes:
a flock of sheep by quiet streams,
Goliath and the Philistines,
the ark brought home, the cheering crowd,
his rise to honor, wealth and fame—
and then he thought of deeds less proud,
of private lust and public shame.

At once the old, repentant king
discerned the theme of his last song:
no hero's epic would he sing
but words of faith, and right and wrong,
what he had learned from forty years
while holding Zion's troubled throne,
the truth distilled from all the fears
and plots and struggles he had known.

He sang that justice is the rain,
and justice is the ripening sun,
and justice gives the growth and gain
which brutal force has never won.
O listen to that ancient king,
you passing rulers, proud and strong!
Heed David's last psalmed whispering
and live the wisdom of his song.

48. Too Splendid for Speech but Ripe for a Song

Too splendid for speech but ripe for a song:
the wonders of God to whom we belong!
What tune can we sing? What rich chords can we play
to honor the potter who made us from clay?

We'll catch the soft sounds that sift from the breeze.
We'll hum with the whales that hum in the seas.
The waters that tickle the earth into spring
will teach us the lilting new life we would sing.

The earth is God's flute, God's cello and chime.
The wind draws the notes. The seasons keep time.
At dusk and at night, from the sunrise past noon
God's playing and singing a ravishing tune.

The swell of earth's praise shall build to a blast
of trumpets and drums when God comes at last
to hear if our lives, like the heavens above,
are filled with the music of justice and love.

Alert to your notes that dance in the heart
we promise, O God, that we'll sing our part
and pray that the song which your song shall inspire
will lead every nation to join in your choir.

49. With Glad, Exuberant Carolings

With glad, exuberant carolings,
with hymns and psalms of praise
give thanks through Christ for everything,
give thanks to God always!
Give thanks through Christ for everything,
give thanks to God always!

Through songful worship know that truth
bare words cannot enfold.
In raptured melodies of prayer
your God behold, behold!
In raptured melodies of prayer
your God behold, behold!

Through music blend the potencies
of mind and heart and soul
and with their fusioned energies
your God extol, extol!
And with their fusioned energies
your God extol, extol!

O brim the barreled lungs with joy
and empty out this song:
"Our breath, our pulse, our lives, our gifts
to Christ, the Lord, belong!
Our breath, our pulse, our lives, our gifts
to Christ, the Lord, belong!"

By day, by night, at work, at prayer,
through storms and times of calm
let all your deeds and words compose
a constant, living psalm!
Let all your deeds and words compose
a constant, living psalm!

50. Startled by a Holy Humming

Startled by a holy humming
drumming in her heart and ear,
Mary heard an angel coming,
Gabriel was drawing near.
From the loud though soundless beating
of the flashing, unseen wings
pulsed the words of sacred greeting:
she would bear the king of kings.

Troubled by the angel's blessing
Mary asked how it could be.
In a way she was confessing
all that doubt can never see:
how the flesh is filled with spirit,
how the heart can beat with love,
how another heart can hear it,
how this comes from God above.

Tending to the voice of heaven
Mary's doubts began to fade
while her faith like rising leaven
grew until she gladly prayed:
"May it be as God has spoken,
may it be as I have heard,
may God's will be never broken,
may I live by God's own word."

Startled, troubled, then believing
Mary's vision opened wide.
She by faith began perceiving
life and truth from heaven's side.
Lord, may we at last like Mary
catch the slant of heaven's light
piercing through the doubts that bury
hope and grace from human sight.

51. Sing with Gabriel the Greeting

Sing with Gabriel the greeting:
"Hail, O Mary, favored one!"
Seek her guidance in completing
all you promised to her son.

Strong enough to question angels
yet compliant to God's way,
now she reigns above archangels
and she hears us when we pray:
As you tended Christ our brother
from the manger to the cross,
keep us faithful, Holy Mother,
through temptation, joy and loss.

Sing with Gabriel . . .

Let the wind that parted oceans
and that stirred the prophets' fire
gather all of our emotions
to a single pure desire
for a life that Christ has entered
and reshaped with grace and love
and like Mary's has been centered
on the will of God above.

Sing with Gabriel . . .

Let the wonder and communion
of the sacred liturgy
that has drawn us into union
with the paschal mystery
amplify the act of praying
to the way we live our days
so our working and our playing
turn to offerings of praise.

Sing with Gabriel . . .

Let the keeping and the living
of our vow and rule and rite
fill us with the grace for giving
vital witness to the light.
From our spiritual formation
may new energies proceed
for the social transformation
of a world in frantic need.

Sing with Gabriel . . .

Let the heritage we're sharing
and the faith tradition feeds
and the dreams our hearts are bearing
make our future words and deeds
worthy of the name we carry
and the hope that name instills:
that our lives will honor Mary
as we do what heaven wills.

Sing with Gabriel . . .

52. God of Gabriel

God of Gabriel,
of birth and life,
hear our prayer:

Like Mary,
make us bold
to question angels.

Like Mary,
help us pray:
Your word be done.

Like Mary,
stir our hearts
to ponder what you do.

Like Mary,
prepare us for
the birth of Christ

53. In the Babble of a Baby

In the babble of a baby
hear life's fundamental prayer:
Abba, Abba, Abba
we are trusting in your care.

Like a mother, like a father
God is parent of us all.
Abba, Abba, Abba
hears and answers when we call.

54. Blessed Be You, O God

Blessed be you, O God
who gave the birds their song,
the whales their hum,
the lions their roar,
and the ocean waves their beat.

Blessed be you for tuning the soul
to the rhythms and songs of praise
that fill your creation.

Blessed be you for poets and prophets
who have honored your word
in ecstatic speech
and faithful proclamation.

Blessed be you
for composers, singers and instrumentalists
who have attended to your Spirit,
drawing music
from the silent hallelujahs of the heart,
shaping breath and sound
to the glory of your name.

Blessed be you for congregations
who have filled their lives with faith
and their voices with song.

Blessed be you for every creature
who joins to proclaim:
How great is your name in all the earth!

55. May the God Whose Music Sounded

May the God whose music sounded
as you led our church and choir
till we knew we were surrounded
by the Spirit's wind and fire
keep singing in your heart
as a witness to Christ's story
and in other souls impart
hymns of Glory, Glory, Glory!

56. Gangling Desert Birds Will Sing

"Gangling desert birds will sing,
jackals too will join God's choir.
Rivers out of rock will spring,
paths will cut through thorn and briar.
In the wilderness of sand
God will lead us by the hand."

"Here and now, in clear, plain view,
God is doing something new!"

"In this strange and foreign land
God in unexpected ways
will do miracles as grand
as the ancient deeds you praise.
God who pushed aside the sea
still redeems and sets us free."

"Here and now, in clear, plain view,
God is doing something new!"

While the exiles far from home
watched their captors' muddy streams
pass between flat banks of loam
Zion's rivers filled their dreams
till Isaiah's words of grace
thundered through that pagan place:

"Here and now, in clear, plain view,
God is doing something new!"

Lord, alert our eyes to probe
with Isaiah's deeper sight
where today upon this globe
you are sowing deeds of light.
Ease our yearning for the past
till we see by faith at last:

"Here and now, in clear, plain view,
God is doing something new!"

A Spendthrift Lover

57. A Spendthrift Lover Is the Lord

A spendthrift lover is the Lord
who never counts the cost
or asks if heaven can afford
to woo a world that's lost.
Our lover tosses coins of gold
across the midnight skies
and stokes the sun against the cold
to warm us when we rise.

Still more is spent in blood and tears
to win the human heart,
to overcome the violent fears
that drive the world apart.
Behold the bruised and thorn-crowned face
of one who bears our scars
and empties out the wealth of grace
that's hinted by the stars.

How shall we love this heart-strong God
who gives us everything,
whose ways to us are strange and odd,
what can we give or bring?
Acceptance of the matchless gift
is gift enough to give.
The very act will shake and shift
the way we love and live.

58. Instead of a King

Instead of a king
who reigns in the skies,
consider a woman
who is brave and wise,
her glory not a crown
but a head of greying hair
and in her voice and face
a kind, perceptive air.

The things that she knows
as lover and friend,
the ways we are broken
and the ways we mend,
the spirit in our hearts,
both the gladness and the pain.
No wonder angels sing:
let this wise woman reign.

59. Holy and Good Is the Gift of Desire

Holy and good is the gift of desire.
God made our bodies for passion and fire,
intending that love would draw from the flame
lives that would shine with God's image and name.

God weeps for all people
abandoned, abused.
God weeps for the women
whose bodies are bruised.
God weeps when the flame
that God has infused
is turned from its purpose
and brutally used.

Holy and good is the gift of desire . . .

God calls to the women,
God calls to the men:
"Don't hide from the terror
or terror will win.
I made you for love,
but love must begin
by facing the violence
without and within."

Holy and good is the gift of desire . . .

God knows that our violence
is mixed with our dust:
God's son was a victim
of violence and lust,
for Jesus revealed
that women will trust
a man who in action
is tender and just.

Holy and good is the gift of desire . . .

60. Far More Than Passion's Passing Flame

Far more than passion's passing flame
has fused our single hearts,
the vow we make in heaven's name
one common future charts.

Through sorrow, joy, temptation, strain,
affliction, rapture, tears,
Lord, let our vows endure and gain
their meaning through the years.

If time dilutes what we feel now
and rich desirings thin,
may we by grace draw from our vow
the strength to love again.

Then at our death, O God, accept
this life-long gift of praise:
the witness of a promise kept
through all our married days.

61. Unbidden Came God's Love

Unbidden came God's love,
not rushing from the skies
as angel, flame or dove
but shining through your eyes.

At first I did not see
that God was there in you—
your love was all to me,
was all I sought and knew.

But then as if the sun
took years and years to dawn
events led one by one
to deeper meanings drawn.

Each time you took my hand,
each time you helped me face
what I could barely stand
God reached to me with grace.

Through these plain common things
rich mysteries I heard:
the fluttering of wings
and God's incarnate word.

62.   Twenty-five Years

Has it been that long?
We don't seem that old.
And why silver, not gold?
To me it's named wrong.

I swear with my heart:
it's been gold from the start.

63. On Bringing a Friend Purple Tulips

It's not because archbishops
and kings who flaunt their powers
are vested in this hue
that I bought these flowers,
but because I dreamed of you
in lavender and morning light
walking through the fields that bloomed
while we talked and talked last night.

A Single Unmatched Stone

64.   A Single Unmatched Stone

A single unmatched stone
the builders hurled aside
holds up the church alone
its cornerstone and pride.
The symmetry the builders planned
was altered by another's hand.

A single faithful act
that healed a man once lame
the temple priests attacked
for bearing Jesus' name.
The righteous heart, the rigid mind
to God's new work were deaf and blind.

A single deed or word
of truth or peace or grace
not seen before or heard
is difficult to face.
Help us, O God, by faith to see
what seems a threat may set us free.

65. The Word of God Was from the Start

The word of God was from the start.
The word drove seas and land apart.
The word made rocks and living things.
The word raised up and brought down kings.

The word became a child of earth.
The word arrived through human birth.
The word like us was blood and bone.
The word knew life as we have known.

The word of God was human-sized,
the word by most unrecognized.
The word by others was received.
The word gave life when they believed.

The word had first made flesh from sod,
the word-made-flesh turned flesh toward God.
The word is working on flesh still.
The word is spelling out God's will.

The word shall be our life and light.
The word shall be our power and might.
The word above all wealth is priced.
The word by name is Jesus Christ.

66. The Hands that First Held Mary's Child

The hands that first held Mary's child
were hard from working wood,
from boards they sawed and planed and filed
and splinters they withstood.
This day they gripped no tool of steel,
they drove no iron nail,
but cradled from the head to heel
our Lord newborn and frail.

When Joseph marveled at the size
of that small breathing frame
and gazed upon those bright new eyes
and spoke the infant's name,
the angel's words he once had dreamed
poured down from heaven's height,
and like the host of stars that beamed
blessed earth with welcome light.

"This child shall be Emmanuel,
not God upon the throne,
but God with us, Emmanuel,
as close as blood and bone."
The tiny form in Joseph's palms
confirmed what he had heard,
and from his heart rose hymns and psalms
for heaven's human word.

The tools which Joseph laid aside
a mob would later lift
and use with anger, fear and pride
to crucify God's gift.
Let us, O Lord, not only hold
the child who's born today,
but charged with faith may we be bold
to follow in his way.

67.   Our Savior's Infant Cries Were Heard

Our savior's infant cries were heard
and met by human love
before he preached one saving word
or prayed to God above.

In Joseph's arms, at Mary's breast,
while Herod's violence spread,
God's love by human love was blessed,
protected, nurtured, fed.

By trusting Christ to human care
God blessed forevermore
the care of children everywhere—
the bruised, the lost, the poor.

Whoever calms a child by night
or guides a youth by day
serves him whose birth by lantern light
was on a bed of hay.

For Christ who was a refugee
from Herod and his sword
is seeking now through us to be
our children's friend and Lord.

68. A Star Not Mapped on Human Charts

A star not mapped on human charts
disturbed the eastern skies
and stirred the questing minds and hearts
of three kings rich and wise.
Attracted by the mystic light
their science did not frame,
they travelled through the cloud of night
to learn its holy name.

That star which cheered the seeking soul
announcing Christ was here,
made Herod plot to keep control
through violence, lies and fear.
The tyrant hid his anxious thought
and said "Report to me
when you have found the child you've sought
that I might come and see."

That star above our shadowed earth
now moved across the skies
and marked the place of holy birth
before the wise men's eyes.
They offered incense, myrrh and gold
while on their knees to pray.
Then through a dream the kings were told:
"Go home another way!"

That star which pierced the ancient night
has faded from above,
yet through the visionary sight
of faith and hope and love
we, like the wisemen, still may find
life's animating goal:
the Christ who prompts the probing mind
and lights the open soul.

69. Neither Desert Wind Nor Sun

Neither desert wind nor sun
nor the wastes of rock and sand
tempted Christ to turn and run
from the trials close at hand.
But his heart began to toss
when the sun was sinking down
and the shadows formed a cross
on the dead and barren ground.

Then came darkness and a cry:
lions roaring on a hill,
prowling with a probing eye
for a sudden, easy kill.
Wakeful through the nervous night
till the break of shadowed day,
Christ would move from faith to fright,
then shift back the other way.

Satan's civil, reasoned voice
traveled on the morning breeze:
"Why the struggle? What's the choice?
It's yourself you have to please."
All the tossing in the night,
all the faith and fright and care
turned to visions of delight
in the dawn's deceiving air.

But the brighter, straighter beams
shining from the midday sun
swept away those easy dreams,
leaving Christ where he'd begun.
Once again the evening came,
followed by the lion's call
day and night and day the same,
forty days and nights in all.

Lord, O Lord, we know the fear
arked upon the shadowed sand,
through the night we still can hear
all the beasts that stalk the land,
and beneath the golden light
of the morning's slanted rays
we are tempted to take flight
from your hard, demanding ways.

In that wild and barren place
where the devil roams about,
where our savior found the grace
stronger than his fear or doubt
give us strength to search and find
what at last he truly knew:
how with heart and soul and mind
we belong, Dear God, to you.

70. To Those Who Knotted Nets of Twine

To those who knotted nets of twine
to comb a fish-filled sea,
Christ called aloud: "Put down that line
and come and follow me!"

Accustomed to the tug of rope
ensnared in rocks and weeds,
they felt from Christ a pull of hope
amidst their tangled needs.

They left their boats, their sails and oars,
but even more than these,
they left the lake's encircling shores
and its familiar breeze.

They braved the tyrant's brutal blast
and hate's unbounded rage,
while rescue lines of faith they cast
to save their sinking age.

O Christ, who called beside the sea,
still call to us today.
Like those who fished in Galilee,
we'll risk your storm-swept way.

CM 86.86   Amazing Grace

71. The Leper's Soul Was No Less Scarred

The leper's soul was no less scarred
than were his face and skin.
The curse, "Unclean, unclean!" had marred
God's image deep within.

No hands had grasped his hands for years,
no lips had kissed his own,
no greeting came his way but jeers
and looks of ice and stone.

Then Jesus stroked the leper's cheek
and swept the sores away
but charged the man he should not speak
of what took place that day.

There was, of course, no way to hold
the news of what Christ did.
The man made sure the tale was told
instead of hushed and hid.

And we who feel Christ's healing hand
can't help but do the same.
The way we speak and walk and stand
will spell our savior's name.

72. We Have the Strength to Lift and Bear

We have the strength to lift and bear
a friend's immobile weight,
the strength to watch and nurse and care
through hours long and late,
because we trust in ways unknown
the springs of health are stirred,
and thus the mind, the flesh and bone
receive Christ's healing word.

It was this hope which filled four men
who carried down the road
a friend whom guilt had gripped within
where life once gladly flowed.
Each foot a stone, each leg a rod,
for years he lay in bed,
in terror of a judging god
and paralyzed by dread.

The awkwardness of matching strides
and one another's pace
while holding up the bed's two sides
to keep their friend in place,
the crowded street, the roof of clay,
the scribe's harsh view of sin—
not all of these could turn away
those stubborn gracious men.

Lord, give your church that single hope
by which those faithful four
could lower down their friend by rope
while others blocked the door.
Though we may lack your gift to heal,
this task is surely ours:
to bring to you the lost who feel
their need of gracious powers.

73. Soundless Were the Tossing Trees

Soundless were the tossing trees,
soundless were the blowing skies,
soundless were the driven leaves—
soundless all before the eyes
of a man who every day
watched the soundless children play
round the soundless, splashing well
near the soundless village bell.

Often he would shape a word
from the feeling in his heart.
Risking what he never heard,
pulling both his lips apart,
blowing hard, he tried to reach
other people's world of speech,
though the sounds he cast in air
often brought a baffled stare.

Then he saw the savior's face,
and he knew his soul was heard,
knew that Christ with tender grace
did not find his groans absurd,
knew as Jesus drew him near
not to flinch away in fear,
but to trust his probing hand
and to read his lips' command.

Earth began to breathe with sound:
wind was swishing in the trees,
leaves were rattling on the ground,
children shouted, giggled, teased
round the singing, splashing well
near the tolling, ringing bell.
He could hear, O he could hear!
And his speech was pure and clear!

Word from whom all words have sprung,
touch my ears and touch my tongue.
Clear the passage to my heart.
Speak within my inward part.
Let your voice as thunder roll
down the canyons of my soul
till your word returns to you,
echoing in all I do.

74. Ballad of the Woman Bent Double

I'd lie in bed if lying still I'd sleep.
But bodies need to turn or they grow sore,
and being bent, just turning is a chore.
Though nights are long, my rest is never deep.

I rise while others walk the world of dreams,
and down my angled back I pull a robe,
then pace the floor until the cock has crowed
and morning light pours in my room in streams.

I haul a pitcher to the village well.
A broken crane that barely hoists its load,
I know each dip and hole that dents the road
and where the frost has made the cobbles swell.

A stranger says today when I am done:
"Look up! The mountain wears a dazzling crown."
But doubled over, I keep looking down
in wave-webbed water searching for the sun.

Arriving home, I hear some skylarks sing.
I guess they're skipping through the air to play.
A friend once drew their course of flight in clay.
"It's like they're climbing stairs to heaven's king.

"Imagine angels bounding up the sky.
They trace in blue the pattern at your feet."
But all I picture listening in the street
are lines in dirt beneath my earthbound eye.

The sabbath falls. I hear a man and child.
"It's time you went to bed. Don't make me scold."
"If God is resting, who is throwing gold?"
"Come in, come in," the father's voice turns mild.

I go to prayers before the others do
and take a place where I can rest and lean.
I'm nodding off. I hope I won't be seen . . .
"Wake up, wake up! The rabbi's calling you."

"What? Who?" They steer me toward the teacher's
hand.
His words surround me—buoyant, soothing, cool.
I feel I'm wading through a healing pool.
His hand unfolds my frame. I stand. I stand!

No sun crowned peak, no skylark's upward track,
no gold that's scattered in the sky by night
will match my praise in breadth or depth or height:
to God alone I'll freely bend my back.

75. Far from the Markets of Rich Meat and Wine

Far from the markets of rich meat and wine
Jesus invited five thousand to dine.
Philip looked out on the crowd and despaired:
fortunes were needed to get things prepared!

Finding a child with two fish and five loaves,
Andrew as well would have sent home the droves,
certain that what would be supper for one,
shared with one another would quickly be done.

Jesus, however, with confident joy
lay his hands over the gifts from the boy,
blessing the giver of fish and of bread,
trusting completely the crowd would be fed.

Out on the hillside, in rows in the grass,
everyone found there was plenty to pass.
And when they gathered what nobody ate,
twelve ample baskets were piled with the weight.

Lest we like Philip and Andrew conclude
we lack enough to give everyone food,
let us each offer what each can afford,
turning together in prayer to the Lord:

Come to this table, Christ. Come and preside.
Touch with your spirit the gifts we provide.
Bless with your presence the breaking of bread,
then we are certain we all shall be fed.

76. What Fabled Names from Judah's Past

What fabled names from Judah's past
did Mary's son receive!
But they whose lips these titles cast
did not yet dare believe:

"You are the Christ! God's holy son,
Messiah, Lord, Anointed One!"

Some called him John while others said
Elijah had returned.
They ranked him with their treasured dead
but none of them discerned:

"You are the Christ! God's holy son,
Messiah, Lord, Anointed One!"

Then heaven opened Peter's mind
and touched it with a flame,
and while the Spirit in him shined
he spoke the Savior's name:

"You are the Christ! God's holy son,
Messiah, Lord, Anointed One!"

But Jesus' words of pain and loss
caused Peter to protest,
he could not fit the nails and cross
with what he had confessed:

"You are the Christ! God's holy son,
Messiah, Lord, Anointed One!"

O Risen Savior, keep us true
to this our boldest claim:
In life and death we'll worship you
and your eternal name:

"You are the Christ! God's holy son,
Messiah, Lord, Anointed One!"

77. A Cheering, Chanting, Dizzy Crowd

A cheering, chanting, dizzy crowd
had stripped the green trees bare
and hailing Christ as king aloud
waved branches in the air.

They laid their garments in the road
and spread his path with palms
and vows of lasting love bestowed
with royal hymns and psalms.

When day dimmed down to deepening dark
the crowd began to fade
till only trampled leaves and bark
were left from the parade.

Lest we be fooled because our hearts
have surged with passing praise,
remind us, God, as this week starts
where Christ has fixed his gaze.

Instead of palms a winding sheet
will have to be unrolled,
a carpet much more fit to greet
the king a cross will hold.

78. Kneeling in the Garden Grass

Kneeling in the garden grass,
Jesus groans against his death,
Let this cup of sorrow pass,
while he prays in that same breath:

Not my will but yours be done.

Soldiers' voices fill the night
and disturb the scented air.
Judas' kiss by lantern light
tests the strength of Jesus' prayer:

Not my will but yours be done.

While the court and priests conspire
how to slant the evidence
Jesus calmly bears their ire
as his prayer grows more intense:

Not my will but yours be done.

We have tasted Peter's tears
when our coward hearts denied
Christ who overcame his fears
when he prayed before he died:

Not my will but yours be done.

We, like Pilate, wash our hands,
keeping order in the streets,
doing what the mob commands
while the blameless Christ repeats:

Not my will but yours be done.

Christ, we weave the crown of thorns
and we place it on your head
when we join the world that scorns
all whose prayer is simply said:

Not my will but yours be done.

While the massive cross of wood
bends and bruises Jesus' frame
hear him seek eternal good
as he prays in Yahweh's name:

Not my will but yours be done.

We with Simon of Cyrene
help the savior bear the cross.
Step by step we slowly glean
what true faith and prayer will cost:

Not my will but yours be done.

 Christ directs the women's tears
toward the coming judgment day
when God weighs our faithless years
with our willingness to pray:

Not my will but yours be done.

While the soldiers throw their dice
they ignore their victim's groans,
lost to them the sacrifice
and the prayer that Jesus moans:

Not my will but yours be done.

One thief snarls an angry sound,
taunting Christ to prove his power,

but the penitent has found
faith and hope to pray this hour:

Not my will but yours be done.

Jesus reads in Mary's eyes
all the sorrow mothers bear,
and he prays his friend supplies
grace to strengthen her own prayer:

Not my will but yours be done.

Jesus gives one loud last cry
at the moment of his death
while his prayer moves heaven's sky
with his final, parting breath:

Not my will but yours be done.

Quiet is the hollowed cave.
Peace and tears and grief descend.
Mourners offer at the grave
what they learned from Christ their friend:

Not my will but yours be done.

79. While the Court and Priests Conspire

While the court and priests conspire
how to slant the evidence
Jesus calmly bears their ire
as his prayer grows more intense:

Not my will but yours be done.

When the massive cross of wood
bends and bruises Jesus' frame
hear him seek eternal good
as he prays in Yahweh's name:

Not my will but yours be done.

Jesus falls beneath the weight
of the cross he's forced to bear
yet its load of sin and hate
do not crush his hope and prayer:

Not my will but yours be done.

Jesus reads in Mary's eyes
all the sorrow mothers bear,
and he prays his friend supplies
grace to strengthen her own prayer:

Not my will but yours be done.

We with Simon of Cyrene
help the savior bear the cross.
Step by step we slowly glean
what true faith and prayer will cost:

Not my will but yours be done.

Seek the courage and the grace
that Veronica displays
when she wipes the bleeding face
of the one who bravely prays:

Not my will but yours be done.

Jesus trips and falls again
as he struggles through the street
where the mob's unceasing din
mocks the prayer his lips repeat:

Not my will but yours be done.

Christ directs the women's tears
toward the coming judgment day
when God weighs our faithless years
with our willingness to pray:

Not my will but yours be done.

Jesus stumbles one last time
nearly broken by the load
yet by prayer finds strength to climb
Calvary's final stretch of road:

Not my will but yours be done.

Naked to the sun and clouds
and the jeers and gawking stare
of the soldiers and the crowds
Christ continues with his prayer:

Not my will but yours be done.

While the soldiers throw their dice
they ignore their victim's groans,
lost to them the sacrifice
and the prayer that Jesus moans:

Not my will but yours be done.

Jesus gives one loud last cry
at the moment of his death
while his prayer moves heaven's sky
with his final, parting breath:

Not my will but yours be done.

As they take the body down
and they wrap it in a sheet
in their hearts they hear the sound
that his lips no more repeat:

Not my will but yours be done.

Quiet is the hollowed cave.
Peace and tears and grief descend.
Mourners offer at the grave
what they learned from Christ their friend:

Not my will but yours be done.

80. Pounding a Nail in My Cellar Shop

Pounding a nail in my cellar shop
with a hammer your father owned,
I hear from the echoing walls when I stop
the music your father intoned

making a stool for his little son
who strained on his toes
to see it all done,
the sawing, the planing, the sharp hammerblows

that rang with a bright steel beat
which the child, grown and wed,
would one day repeat
building his daughter the small wood sled

now leaning against my cellar wall
as a sign that the past
which the echoes recall
is as true as the nail I am pounding fast,

as true as a stool or a sled
or the sound of a hammered board
or a cup of wine and some broken bread
and the call of your carpenter Lord.

81. Crucified Savior

Crucified Savior,
when we sing of Calvary
we hear a hammer pounding nails,
we see a reddened hill
underneath a darkened sky,
and we shudder to remember
your uncompromising words,
Take up your cross and follow me.

Then with the psalmist we wonder:
Where can we flee from your presence?
Where can we hide
from your demanding spirit,
from the strenuous work of love,
from the severities of doing justice
in a brutal world?

Risen Lord,
Forgive our betrayal,
our running away,
our lack of courage,
our failure of nerve.
Infuse us with a passionate faith
until we seek no other glory
than what lies past Calvary's hill
and our living and our dying
and our rising by your will. Amen.

82. No Iron Spike, No Granite Weight

No iron spike, no granite weight,
no mob aroused and crazed by hate
could seal in stone to lasting death
the Christ who is our life and breath.

Two nights he lay beneath the earth,
a hollowed rock his borrowed berth.
Two nights it seemed death ruled the land,
two nights and then death lost command.

Before dawn's mists could wreathe and coil
and lift the scent of clay and soil,
God's finger poked aside the stone,
and Christ arose to take his throne.

Three women came to honor Christ
with pungent oils of herbs and spice.
Instead they found this startling sight:
a young man sitting robed in white.

The words he spoke to Jesus' friends
are words of hope that God still sends
to those who grieve beside the grave
and ask if God can really save:

"The one you seek does not lie here.
Walk out in faith and not in fear,
and you will see beyond your loss
to Christ who lives despite the cross."

83. Set Free, Set Free by God's Grace

Set free, set free by God's grace!
Unbound, unbound, my heart sings
With joy, with joy that Christ brings
The love that shines from God's face.

Yes, Jesus, Jesus freed me
with love, with love,
when fear and doubt had seized me.

As one who hears a child's cries
And runs to meet the child's needs,
God hears and tends our deep sighs
Not counting works and good deeds.

Yes, Jesus, Jesus freed me
with love, with love,
when fear and doubt had seized me.

As rain has made the world green
So grace has brought to new birth
New hearts, new minds—a new earth!
Old debts and sins are swept clean.

Yes, Jesus, Jesus freed me
with love, with love,
when fear and doubt had seized me.

The highest wall that sin builds
Can't bank the tide of love's flood
Nor stop the grace that God wills
That flows from Christ with Christ's blood.

Yes, Jesus, Jesus freed me
with love, with love,
when fear and doubt had seized me.

Christ welcomes you as his guest.
He knows you walk a long road
And bend beneath a hard load.
In Christ, in Christ you'll find rest.

Yes, Jesus, Jesus freed me
with love, with love,
when fear and doubt had seized me.

Though bright as blood be our sin
Christ's blood transforms the deep stain.
What all our work cannot win
Christ's grace and mercy can gain.

Yes, Jesus, Jesus freed me
with love, with love,
when fear and doubt had seized me.

Because the love the Lord's shown
Has claimed my life as Christ's own
My house and I have one aim:
To live the praise of God's name.

Yes, Jesus, Jesus freed me
with love, with love,
when fear and doubt had seized me.

84.   Our Shepherd Is the Lamb

Our shepherd is the lamb—
let no more blood be shed!
But love and serve the great I Am
and feast on wine and bread.

The world the snake beguiles
will doubt our hymn is true
unless the love that reconciles
is plain in all we do.

Our shepherd is the lamb . . .

Each time we drop the stones
our angry hearts would toss
we show the world that Christ atones
and saves us by the cross.

Our shepherd is the lamb . . .

By lives of peace and grace
that do not bend to wrong
we gather others to this place
to join us in our song:

Our shepherd is the lamb . . .

Behold how Calvary's tree
is leafing in the sky
and roots itself in hearts which see
that sin and death shall die.

Our shepherd is the lamb . . .

85. How Unlike All Earthly Glory

How unlike all earthly glory
is the glory that we sing,
moved to worship by the story
of the slaughtered lamb our king,
who in ways beyond our knowing
comes as manna from above,
and as wine that's poured and flowing
from the very heart of love.

How unlike all earthly glory
is the glory that we sing,
moved to worship by the story
of the slaughtered lamb our king,
who awakens our devotion
as the living pulse and breath
of the prayer he sets in motion
through his sacrificial death.

How unlike all earthly glory
is the glory that we sing,
moved to worship by the story
of the slaughtered lamb our king,
who provides us while we're kneeling
what we lose our selves to find:
the profoundest sense of healing
that can touch the heart and mind.

How unlike all earthly glory
is the glory that we sing,
moved to worship by the story
of the slaughtered lamb our king,
whom we meet through interaction
with the holy sacrament
that renews our strength for action
when our energies are spent.

How unlike all earthly glory
is the glory that we sing,
moved to worship by the story
of the slaughtered lamb our king!

86. Crown as Your King the King Who Came Crownless

Crown as your king, the king who came crownless,
challenging Pilate's imperious ways.
Crown as your sovereign Christ whose love is boundless.
Crown him with prayer and with praise!

Emblazon upon your heart
the cross and the crimsoned crown,
the signs of your humble king
whose splendid grace the heavens sing.

Crown him whose crown was brambles and nettles,
knotted by hands that were hardened to pain.
Crown him whose gospel constantly unsettles
systems of tyrannous reign.

Emblazon upon your heart
the cross and the crimsoned crown,
the signs of your humble king
whose splendid grace the heavens sing.

Crown as your king the king of compassion.
Serve as his envoy of justice and love.
Fill your commission: faithfully refashion
earth to the kingdom above.

Emblazon upon your heart
the cross and the crimsoned crown,
the signs of your humble king
whose splendid grace the heavens sing.

Crown him with hymns instead of with briars.
Crown him the sovereign to whom you belong.
Crown him with worship. Braid with heaven's choirs
garlands of music and song.

Emblazon upon your heart
the cross and the crimsoned crown,
the signs of your humble king
whose splendid grace the heavens sing.

Fragmentary Prayers

87. Through Our Fragmentary Prayers

Through our fragmentary prayers
and our silent, heart-hid sighs
wordlessly the Spirit bears
our profoundest needs and cries.

Deeper than the pulse's beat
is the Spirit's speechless groan,
making human prayers complete
through the prayer that is God's own.

Let our jabberings give way
to the hummings in the soul
as we yield our lives this day
to the God who makes us whole.

Search and sound our mind and heart,
Breath and Flame and Wind and Dove,
let your prayer in us impart
strength to do the work of love.

88. The Branch that Bends with Clustered Fruit

The branch that bends with clustered fruit
still needs the pruner's blade
to keep it close to vine and root
or else its strength will fade.

The spindly, twisted, tangled coil
of branches overgrown
produces nothing from its toil
but feeds itself alone.

The pruner's hook will gently play
where fruitful growth is seen
but like an axe will slash away
the empty net of green.

O God, who fills with rain and sun
the grapes we press for wine,
cut off the growth our fears have spun
and prune us to your vine.

89. Before the Fruit Is Ripened by the Sun

Before the fruit is ripened by the sun,
before the petals or the leaves uncoil,
before the first fine silken root is spun,
a seed is dropped and buried in the soil.
Before the Easter Alleluias ring,
before the massive rock is rolled aside,
before the fear of death has lost its sting,
a just and loving man is crucified.

Before we gain the grace that comes through loss,
before we live by more than bread and breath,
before we lift in joy an empty cross,
we face with Christ the seed's renewing death.

90. Let All Who Pray the Prayer Christ Taught

Let all who pray the prayer Christ taught
first clear the cluttered heart.
Make room to breathe the living thought
those well-worn words impart.

Dismiss the fear that this world drifts
with no one in command.
Your pulse and breath are signs and gifts
from God's attentive hand.

Refine and test each passing aim
against this final one:
has your life hallowed heaven's name
and has God's will been done?

Discard each vengeful hope that's fed
the dreams of wars you'll win,
then freely ask for daily bread
and pardon from your sin.

Examine how temptation breeds
inside the mind's dark maze,
acknowledging that your life needs
deliverance from its ways.

By faithful discipline prepare
an inward holy space
that when you offer Jesus' prayer
your heart may fill with grace.

91. Creator of All That Is

Creator of all that is
we are not
what you made us to be.

If our sin is pride
remind us
every breath
is a gift from you.

If our sin is humility
remind us
we are made
in your image.

If our sin is the neglect of our souls
remind us
you are praying
through our sighs
too deep for words.

If our sin is neglect of others
remind us
Christ speaks
through cries of human need.

Whatever our sin
remind us
your mercy is endless
for those who love you,
and we can be a new creation
through Jesus Christ.

92. Seek Not in Distant, Ancient Hills

Seek not in distant, ancient hills
the promised holy land
but where you live do what God wills
and find it close at hand.

A single heaven wraps around
this whirling, watered stone,
and every place is sacred ground
where God is loved and known.

To climb the templed, footworn peak
where pilgrims long have trod
unlock the bolted soul and seek
the present, living God.

In spirit and in truth you'll find
what human thought can't frame:
the source of breath and pulse and mind,
the primal wind and flame.

93. As a Chalice Cast of Gold

As a chalice cast of gold,
burnished, bright and brimmed with wine,
make me, Lord, as fit to hold
grace and truth and love divine.
Let my praise and worship start
with the cleansing of my heart.

Save me from the soothing sin
of the empty cultic deed
and the pious, babbling din
of the claimed but unlived creed.
Let my actions, Lord, express
what my tongue and lips profess.

When I bend upon my knees,
clasp my hands or bow my head,
let my spoken, public pleas
be directly, simply said,
free of tangled words that mask
what my soul would plainly ask.

When I dance or chant your praise,
when I sing a song or hymn,
when I preach your loving ways,
let my heart add its Amen.
Let each cherished, outward rite
thus reflect your inward light.

94. Searcher of Human Hearts

Searcher of human hearts,
we join those who in every age
have prayed for a new heart
and a right spirit.

We join Isaiah,
confessing
our hearts are often far from you.

We join the Psalmist,
offering
a broken and a contrite heart.

We join Ezekiel,
asking
hearts of stone become hearts of flesh.

We join Mary,
pondering
in our hearts the meaning of Christ.

We join Paul,
hoping
Christ may dwell in our hearts by faith.

We join these prayers into one,
trusting
you will bring from new hearts
deeds of justice and love,
awakening
faith and hope
in hearts that have not known you.

95. Forever in the Heart There Springs

Forever in the heart there springs
a hunger never touched by things,
and if unmet, this inward need
goes prowling as incessant greed:
we reach and reach for more and more
while with each gain we still seem poor.
We work to earn what can't be bought;
through prayer and faith it must be sought.

True Bread of Heaven, Life Divine,
Eternal Manna, Holy Sign,
our need of you incites our quest,
your presence brings our search to rest:
the hollow, hungry heart is filled
and all its grasping motions stilled,
our quenchless thirst is satisfied,
and every need and want supplied.

Let Christ be praised forevermore
who makes us rich when we are poor,
who sees the tattered, begging soul
beneath the cloak of class and role,
who hears the heart's unspoken groan
and meets our need as if his own,
to whom all thirst and hunger yield,
the bread whose taste is truth revealed.

96.   If All You Want, Lord, Is My Heart

If all you want, Lord, is my heart,
my heart is yours alone—
providing I may set apart
my mind to be my own.

If all you want, Lord, is my mind,
my mind belongs to you,
but let my heart remain inclined
to do what it would do.

If heart and mind would both suffice,
while I kept strength and soul,
at least I would not sacrifice
completely my control.

But since, O God, you want them all
to shape with your own hand,
I pray for grace to heed your call
to live your first command.

97. Heart, Hold Fast

Heart, hold fast.
One truth clasp:

Center on Christ alone.
On Christ alone.
Christ alone.
Christ.

Mind, be still.
Do God's will:

Center on Christ alone.
On Christ alone.
Christ alone.
Christ.

Soul, drive deep.
One thought keep:

Center on Christ alone.
On Christ alone.
Christ alone.
Christ.

Church, bow low.
One faith know:

Center on Christ alone.
On Christ alone.
Christ alone.
Christ.

World, draw near.
One word hear:

Center on Christ alone.
On Christ alone.
Christ alone.
Christ.

98.   On a Visit South in January

If winter never spiked and stunned
muscles which the summer sunned
and did not force the blood's retreat
from fingers, hands, toes and feet
until they felt from skin to bone
less like flesh and more like stone,

but if instead, all winds were soft
and gently bore my breath aloft
and if I walked for all my days
warm through seas of warming rays,
I might believe that I was soul,
and sky, not earth, my final goal.

I hope this visit soon will end.
I need a cold and raging wind.
The winter of my northern clime
is for me rehearsal time:

all my joints that bend and fold
hinge the way they will when old,
my long legs learn in knee-high snow
how their stride will shrink and slow,
the lungs that barrel hard sharp air
practice how to breathe with care,

and most of all, my chambered heart
tries its final fading part.

99.   Unless This Day Be Holy

Unless this day be holy
all days shall blur to one,
as orderly but empty
they march from sun to sun.
But if we keep the Sabbath
through prayer and song and praise,
we'll find the sacred meaning
of all our working days.

Our worship, like the lightning
that lifts the curtained night,
shall cast before us shining
what darkness hides from sight:
the wonder and the glory
we dimly sense and feel,
the circling sacred presence
our busy lives conceal.

O let this day be holy
and rich in strength and peace,
and when the day is over
its meaning shall increase,
as day by day we labor
to shape our work and art
to fit the holy visions
that thunder in out heart.

100.   Beyond the Press and Pull of Crowds

Beyond the press and pull of crowds
who needed him by day,
Christ found beneath the moon-rimed clouds
a lonely place to pray.

The hands which straightened angled bones
he lifted to the sky,
and with the Spirit's wordless groans
he called to God on high.

The ragged world's raw, restless need
flowed upward to the sky,
and strength to heal, to teach and feed
the Spirit resupplied.

When night at last began to thin,
he sensed upon the air
the busy day's approaching din,
its work and weight and wear.

But greater still, he felt deep down
the soul's resilient power.
The lift of hope no grief can drown
had been renewed that hour.

Lord, lead us to a lonely place
where we by night may pray
and then, like Christ, arise to face
the cries and needs of day.

101. When Heaven's Voice Was Still

When heaven's voice was still
and holy visions rare,
young Samuel sought to do God's will
and lived by faith and prayer.

Beside the temple ark,
beneath the sacred flame,
he heard one night within the dark
a voice that called his name.

Three times that night he woke.
Three times to Eli came.
Three times and then he knew God spoke
and summoned him by name.

Once more, O God, it seems
your living word is rare.
Speak now to us in holy dreams
and visions born of prayer.

And if your voice is missed
or weakly, wrongly heard,
we pray then, Lord, persist, persist
until we grasp your word.

102. Before the Temple's Great Stone Sill

Before the great stone sill
was quarried, smoothed and squared,
a dreaming prophet glimpsed God's will
and heaven's word declared.

"Our tenting Lord who guides and calls
has never sought a home.
God will not be enclosed by walls.
God wants to move and roam."

If Nathan's words inform our praise
and all the prayers we frame,
our worship then will leap and blaze
with God's confineless flame.

But if we clutch with heart and hand
the symbols we have made
as though they were God's first command,
our prayer and song will fade.

Grant, Lord, your church a tenting soul,
not tied to wood or stone,
but fixed for ever on this goal:
the praise of you alone.

103. All that Rises toward the Sky

All that rises toward the sky,
mist and smoke and breath and haze,
marks before the faithful eye
prayer's ascending path of praise:

While the cloud of incense lifts,
bless us, Christ, as living gifts.

Here before the sacrament
that has drawn our hearts above
we renew our best intent
to embody grace and love.

While the cloud of incense lifts,
bless us, Christ, as living gifts.

As the haze and mist return
to the earth as welcome showers,
at the altar we discern
prayer restores our vital powers.

While the cloud of incense lifts,
bless us, Christ, as living gifts.

All that rises from the earth
through the purifying air
joins the cycle of rebirth
that continues in our prayer:

While the cloud of incense lifts,
bless us Christ as living gifts.

104.   The Scantest Touch of Grace Can Heal

The scantest touch of grace can heal
a wound that's bled for years
if first we dare to reach and feel
beyond our pain and tears.

Observe a hand stretched out to brush
the hem of Jesus' gown.
That bleeding woman trusts one touch
will make her body sound.

She cannot see the savior's face,
but lunges for his robe:
at once a surge of healing grace
where stubborn blood has flowed.

Like her, O Christ, we reach for you.
One touch is all we need.
We stretch for grace to make us new
and heal our wounds that bleed.

105. A Fixed Sum

In shade I watched my neighbor in the sun:
Karl gripped his hand mower and started at a run,
but seven steps later he had already slowed
so the blade stopped whirring and no longer mowed,
allowing the roller to mat the grass down.

Karl had bought the antique at a yard sale in town.
He called it, "One of your old-fashioned deals.
It's got a handle of oak and cast iron wheels.
The owner asked twelve. I got it for nine.
Sharpened and oiled, it ought to cut fine."
That had been back in the first days of May,
when—after five months shoveling—mowing was play.
But sweating and panting in late August heat,
Karl cursed the green that grew at his feet.
Once before, in the middle of July,
after heavy rain, when the grass was high
(though compared to now it might have been lower)
I offered to loan him my rotary mower.
"No thanks," he said, then braced his feet against the ground
and forced from his mower a motorized sound.
I thought of Karl's edger I often used,
pliers and wrenches he never refused:
"Feel free to borrow whatever you need."
As I watched him straining to keep up his speed,
I saw that his words only applied
when he was on the giving side.

Yet he might agree to use what I own
if it looked like a swap, not like a loan.
Before offering the mower I first must ask
for a hard-to-find tool for a hard-to-do-task.
What did I need to repair or replace?
What I needed most was storage space.

Karl had a shed where he puttered around,
a shop that to him was sacred ground.
But I lacked a barn, a garage or a shed
and kept my tools in the cellar instead—
which is fine for pitchforks, shovels and hoes
or anything light that handles like those.

But a machine that takes two to haul outdoors,
that dribbles gas on the stairs and floors
was often enough to keep me away
from my tiny lawn (though it grew like hay).
That hot August day when his blade would not cut
and each iron wheel packed the grass in a rut,
Karl rolled his mower into his shed.
His shoulders were stooped and he hung his head.
I waited for dusk, when back from my walk,
we had our usual summer night talk
about too little sun and much too much rain
(which had dammed with debris an outside drain).
Then, when the ritual chatter had ended,
I said to him what I really intended:
"Lugging my mower upstairs is a chore—
the thing spills gas and it makes my back sore.
You wouldn't have room in your shed to spare?"
He closed his eyes and thought with great care.
Then he looked at me straight: "I'll check if I do."
He returned to announce what he already knew:
"There's room between my bench and the sink.
Look for yourself and see what you think."
"I'm sure it'll do. But I ought to pay rent.
Free use of my mower for the space you've lent?"
The grass in his yard was beginning to stand.
He nodded yes and gave me his hand.

I awake today to a September dawn
and notice I need to cut my lawn.

I wait for the sun to burn off the dew.
When I enter Karl's shed, my mower looks new,
he's wiped off the oil and cleaned off the grass.
I check the fuel: he's filled it with gas.
I thought we had made a simple swap:
use of my mower for space in his shop.
But despite the rent to store it inside,
I guess Karl felt on the receiving side.
I don't know the word I'd use to his face,
but I think we're lacking what once was called "grace."
It's what he sensed in a mechanical way
when he brought the hand mower home in May
and took off the rust and sharpened the blade,
admiring its weight and the way it was made:

"They did not skimp with the metal or wood.
They used the best they possibly could."
Oiling the bearings, he named what we've lost:
"It seems they didn't keep track of the cost."

I roll out the mower that's no longer mine—
it comes from Karl's shop, it's got a store shine.
I start the thing up and walk straight ahead.
Karl waves while he weeds in his flower bed.
Neighbors already, what friends we'd become
if giving and taking were not a fixed sum,
with fifty percent in each account
and no way to vary either amount.

106. Silence! Frenzied, Unclean Spirit

"Silence! Frenzied, unclean spirit,"
cried God's healing, holy One.
"Cease your ranting!
Flesh can't bear it.
Flee as night before the sun."
At Christ's voice the demon trembled,
from its victim madly rushed,
while the crowd that was assembled
stood in wonder, stunned and hushed.

Lord, the demons still are thriving
in the grey cells of the mind:
tyrant voices shrill and driving,
twisted thoughts that grip and bind,
doubts that stir the heart to panic,
fears distorting reason's sight,
guilt that makes our loving frantic,
dreams that cloud the soul with fright.

Silence, Lord, the unclean spirit,
in our mind and in our heart.
Speak your word that when we hear it
all our demons shall depart.
Clear our thought and calm our feeling,
still the fractured, warring soul.
By the power of your healing
make us faithful, true and whole.

107. Wherever There Are Tyrant Voices

Leader: Wherever there are tyrant voices breeding hatred and prejudice,

People: Silence, Lord, the unclean spirit.

Leader: Wherever fear is paralyzing the capacity to do justice and show compassion,

People: Silence, Lord, the unclean spirit.

Leader: Wherever human souls are depressed and divided and at war with themselves,

People: Silence, Lord, the unclean spirit.

Leader: Wherever nations are driven by forces of exploitation and op-pression.

People: Silence, Lord, the unclean spirit.

Leader: Wherever people are afraid to call on your name because of doubt or lack of freedom,

People: Silence, Lord, the unclean spirit.

Leader: Wherever hostility is fueling abuse and mindless violence,

People: Silence, Lord, the unclean spirit.

108. Ask, Seek, Knock

Ask,
seek,
knock.
When you think your life is closed,
name what you have presupposed
and examine it by prayer.
Ask,
seek,
knock:
who's creating your despair?

Ask,
seek,
knock.
Doors that doubt has left untried
searching faith can open wide.

Ask,
seek,
knock.
When you contemplate the night
knowing every point of light
is a distant blazing sun,
ask,
seek,
knock:
why was all of this begun?

Ask,
seek,
knock.
Doors that doubt has left untried
searching faith can open wide.

Ask,
seek,
knock.

When belief's initial seed
and your early childhood creed
are the only faith you know,
ask,
seek,
knock:
have you faith to let faith grow?

Ask,
seek,
knock.
Doors that doubt has left untried
searching faith can open wide.

Ask,
seek,
knock.
When you see the hollow eyes
and the stooped and shrunken size
of a people needing bread,
ask,
seek,
knock:
why are others overfed?

Ask,
seek,
knock.
Doors that doubt has left untried
searching faith can open wide.

Ask,
seek,
knock.
When your ponderings persist
as a voice you can't resist
and you wonder what to do,
ask,
seek,
knock:
is it Christ who's calling you?

Ask,
seek,
knock.
Doors that doubt has left untried
searching faith can open wide.

109. O Gracious Christ

O gracious Christ,
you come seeking us.
We hear your knock upon the door
through the voice of the stranger,
through the cry for food and shelter,
through the hunger in our souls
and the visions in our hearts.

Startled and afraid,
we refuse to answer
and leave the door shut.

Forgive our lack of hospitality.
Make us as gracious as you are,
eager to receive you
in one another
and to share our meal together.

Then you, our welcome guest,
will be our host instead,
and we will answer every time
you knock upon the door.

Disturbance of the Solid Ground

110. Where Mountains Lift the Eye

Where mountains lift the eye
above the level plain
and stretch our sight toward heaven's sky
we work and pray to gain
a vision of the range
that rises in the mind
as science, thought and culture change
how faith will be defined.

We do not fear
for we believe
God dreams of worlds
we can't conceive.

The highest peaks are found
where plates of bedrock shift.
Disturbance of the solid ground
is God's creative gift,
who still is sculpting earth
and uses that same art
around the world to bring to birth
new landscapes in the heart.

We do not fear
for we believe
God dreams of worlds
we can't conceive.

Those lofty, sharp edged forms
attract the clouds and rain
and with their melting winter storms
revive the thirsting plain
where seeds then burst and sprout
with the same urgent force
that turns a barren heart from doubt
to praise life's end and source.

We do not fear
for we believe
God dreams of worlds
we can't conceive.

As primal powers fuse
earth's drifting crust of stone,
the stress of many creeds and views
far different from our own
will not destroy belief
but make it broad and wise
and faith's familiar old relief
will see new mountains rise.

We do not fear
for we believe
God dreams of worlds
we can't conceive.

111. God Folds the Mountains Out of Rock

God folds the mountains out of rock
and fuses elemental powers
in ores and atoms we unlock
to claim as if their wealth were ours.
From veins of stone we lift up fire,
and too impressed by our own skill
we use the flame that we acquire
not thinking of the Maker's will.

Our instruments can probe and sound
the folded mountain's potent core,
but wisdom's ways are never found
among the lodes of buried ore,
yet wisdom is the greater need,
and wisdom is the greater source,
for lacking wisdom we proceed
to waste God's other gifts on force.

Lord, grant us what we cannot mine,
what science cannot plumb or chart:
your wisdom and your truth divine
enfolded in a faithful heart.
Then we like mountains richly veined
will be a source of light and flame
whose energies have been ordained
to glorify the Maker's name.

112. The Least in God's Kingdom Is Greater than John

The least in God's kingdom is greater than John
for God is not founding the kingdom upon
the standards we use to determine and gauge
who ranks with the greatest and least of our age.

The world in which people and nations are classed
and property, privilege, and profits dispersed
according to wealth and its systems of caste
will be in the kingdom completely reversed.

A shift in the world has already begun
through wonders and healings that Jesus has done
among those not favored by riches or birth
yet bearing God's image of infinite worth.

Christ, topple the ladder of arrogant thought
we climb in our struggle for status and gain
that we may embody the kingdom you brought
through love that transfigures injustice and pain.

113. The Christians Traveled Caesar's Roads

The Christians traveled Caesar's roads,
and as the Spirit led,
they stopped to carry strangers' loads
and share their faith and bread.
By simple acts the word was sown
and spread from place to place
till highways of the Roman throne
became a web of grace.

Then past the reach of Caesar's Rome,
cross deserts, mountains, ice,
the word moved on and found a home
in all who welcomed Christ.
They carved in stone and traced in glass
the stories they received
to help their children's children grasp
the gospel they believed.

But hallowed walls could not contain
the Spirit's growing storm,
the wind whose gathered force ordained
the church's full reform
and sent the word around the globe
to kindle and ignite
new fires of faith to warm and robe
the world in greater light.

The word that traveled Caesar's roads
and raised cathedral spires
still calls to us and lifts our loads
and stirs the Spirit's fires,
and gives us daily cause for praise
and sends us from this place
directing us to seek new ways
to weave a web of grace.

114. The Faith We Sing Was Sown

The faith we sing was sown
by ancestors believing
that what we work to own
we are in fact receiving.
They thanked the Lord for soil,
for rain and sun and air
and graced their lives of toil
through sacrament and prayer.

Give thanks for sturdy love
that did not fade and falter
but drew from God above
new strength around the altar.
Give thanks for all those years
the church has broken bread,
and hope replaced our fears
because our faith was fed.

Give thanks the past imparts
this sacred time of favor
to fix within our hearts
a faith that will not waiver,
to wait upon and heed
the Spirit's inward call,
to show by word and deed
that Christ is Lord of all.

We bear with Christ the task
for which he was anointed.
The Spirit now is cast
on us whom he appointed:
to bring the poor good news,
to break the captives' chains,
to heal the heart's deep bruise
and see that justice reigns.

Lord, make this jubilee
a time of clear decision
when we courageously
proclaim and live your vision.
Then from our witness bring
to ages yet unknown
the confidence to sing
the faith that we have sown.

115. Our Founders Cleared an Open Field

Our founders cleared an open field
in thick and tangled wood
and built this church whose lines revealed
faith plainly understood:
clear windows letting in the light,
a pulpit, table, spire,
the simplest things to make more bright
what filled their hearts with fire.

Christ the source and center
of all our nights and days
welcomes you to enter
this house of prayer and praise.

The steeple on the village green
by lifting eyes above
moved hearts to find the link between
belief and work and love.
And still it draws our line of sight
toward that profounder view
which judges by unshaded light
the sum of all we do.

Christ the source and center
of all our nights and days
welcomes you to enter
this house of prayer and praise.

We cannot count the wealth of prayer
or add the total worth
of all the hope and acts of care
this church has given birth.
Yet we are heirs of those who found
new strength for loving here,
and when we meet our praises sound
the faith their lives made clear.

Christ the source and center
of all our nights and days
welcomes you to enter
this house of prayer and praise.

Earth is the village green we share,
a mossy stone in space,
whose sight awakes our founders' prayer
for faith to live by grace
lest we assume the world is ours
and treat it as our own
when all the planet's vital powers
belong to God alone.

Christ the source and center
of all our nights and days
welcomes you to enter
this house of prayer and praise.

116. The Cross on the Hill Is the Measuring Rod

The cross on the hill is the measuring rod
that plumbs to the limit
our sin and pretension,
and marks where they meet
that profounder dimension:
the measureless depths of the mercy of God.

We hold up our lives to the cross on the hill
and trace in our history
the tragic declension
of justice and love
and our finest intention
that all that we do would embody God's will.

O Christ, we are stunned by the span of our sin
that shadows our knowledge,
our art and invention,
but thanks to your grace
that is past comprehension
new life and new love and new worlds will begin.

117. The Beauty of the Sound of the Bells

The beauty of the sound of the bells
rings from a tower
that rises from a building
that houses a school
that teaches a tradition
that grows from a history
that flows with the blood
of slaves who were chained
and women who were silenced
as the church gave witness
to Christ who inspired
the people who built
the tower that rings
with the beauty of the sound of the bells.

118. The Rocks Would Shout if We Kept Still

The rocks would shout if we kept still
and failed to preach the word.
It is the Lord's insistent will
the truth be told and heard.

We're called to speak disturbing things
though wealth and power conspire
to hush the messenger who brings
God's purifying fire.

The rocks would shout . . .

We're called to bear with grace the scorn
of hearts so often bruised
that when we tell of hope reborn
they fear to trust the news.

The rocks would shout . . .

We're called to preach by Jesus Christ
who with the Spirit's breath
will make our fragile words suffice
to raise new life from death.

The rocks would shout . . .

119. These Things Did Thomas Count as Real

These things did Thomas count as real:
the warmth of blood, the chill of steel,
the grain of wood, the heft of stone,
the last frail twitch of flesh and bone.

The vision of his skeptic mind
was keen enough to make him blind
to any unexpected act
too large for his small world of fact.

His reasoned certainties denied
that one could live when one had died,
until his fingers read like braille
the markings of the spear and nail.

May we, O God, by grace believe
and thus the risen Christ receive,
whose raw imprinted palms reached out
and beckoned Thomas from his doubt.

120.   I Walk the Farm I Never Walked

I open the black cupboard door, a single wide warped plank,
and from the shelved dark drifts the smell of sour wood.
I rub where the door rubbed before it shrank
then stand in the barn where I never stood
and walk the farm I never walked
though I made many visits when Grandmother talked:

"Two summers in a row the rain had drowned the crop
and made in every field and yard a river, lake or pool.
After which it rained some more, then still refused to stop.
So my sister had to take the offer from the boarding school,
which wrote her back: For the attic dorm each teacher brings
a cupboard, wide as a single bed, to store her private things.

"Father gathered planks he'd laid to walk across the muck.
(Water stains and boot prints hide beneath those coats of
black.)
If I had cash from beans, he said, If I had better luck,
I'd make no cupboard out of boards that when they dry will
crack.
The wood kept drinking paint they way it had been drinking
rain.
Once it downed the can, it still was showing grain.
"Those rough unfinished spots Rosalia did not mind,
But the smell of barnyard boards she feared would fill the
dorm.
She fixed up pomanders from cloves pressed into orange rind
to hide the heavy air of wood and earth and storm.
When all the crops were rotted, September came in fine,
and Rosalia rode to school with her cupboard made of pine."

The cupboard sits in my house now. I smell the flooded yard,
and I am glad for rains my family cursed,
that saved for me the things they would discard.
I rub the cupboard, tap the boards and thirst
to touch and see beneath the paint the wood they touched and saw,
to let my fingers read like braille each crack and knot and flaw.

I brush on stripper, brace my weight against my putty knife
and scrape across the top. Black comes off revealing black.
I scrape and scrape as if were buried underneath a life
I had to free. The paint first yields to my attack
a blade-wide strip of wood. I scrape still more. Then next I sand—
with every stroke I'm traveling back to see my family's land.

I place the cupboard in the hall where people leave their wraps.
Four coats of linseed oil have made the dead wood glow.
Often as my guests come in they give it rubs and pats,
and when they put their coats back on they ask before they go:
"Is that a family treasure?" Yes, I nod, then drift away
to field and farm and family the rain has turned to clay.

121. Risen Christ, May Death Be Swift

Risen Christ, may death be swift
for a friend whose fight is done—
not as winter dusk
bleeding darkened light
from a vanished sun,

not as slow as your own death
but as swift as your last prayer,
"Abba, I commend
all I am to you
trusting in your care,"

and as swift as earth to thrill
when God's trumpet breaks the skies
and restored by you
all our broken flesh
healed and whole shall rise.

122.   How Long, O Lord, How Long?

How long, O Lord, how long?
The ancient cry is ours.
We wait in grief and ask how long
before we feel your powers.

And why, O Lord, and why?
We ask with every age
and throw against your distant sky
the force of grief and rage.

The cross, O Lord, the cross!
We think upon your son:
you know the weight and edge of loss,
your tears and ours are one.

Your hand, O Lord, your hand!
We need your hand to hold,
to walk this dark, uncharted land
where solid meanings fold.

We trust, O Lord, we trust
in time our grief shall mend,
transformed by love that shaped our dust,
your love that knows no end.

123.   View the Present through the Promise

View the present through the promise,
Christ will come again.
Trust despite the deepening darkness,
Christ will come again.
Lift the world above its grieving
through your watching and believing
in the hope past hope's conceiving:
Christ will come again.

Probe the present with the promise,
Christ will come again.
Let your daily actions witness,
Christ will come again.
Let your loving and your giving
and your justice and forgiving
be a sign to all the living:
Christ will come again.

Match the present to the promise,
Christ will come again.
Make this hope your guiding premise,
Christ will come again.
Pattern all your calculating
and the world you are creating
to the advent you are waiting:
Christ will come again.

124. Fierce the Force that Curled Cain's Fist

Fierce the force that curled Cain's fist—
would he master it or yield?
Thick the bitter, weeping mist
rising from the reddened field.
God, whose love for love alone
shaped us deep in Eden's shade,
wept to see what Cain had sown
in the earth that heaven made.

Abel's blood is crying still,
crying, crying from the ground
while the heirs of Cain yet kill
and the pleas of earth are drowned.
But the hearts that fashion death
beat as well with holy dreams,
from the source of pulse and breath
springs a vision that redeems:

Every fist an open hand,
every sword a pruner's blade,
every bomb in every land
to a plow or tractor made,
every raging soul like Cain's
with the grace of God infused
that the passion in the veins
may for peaceful ends be used.

We confess we are Cain's heirs,
that the violent heart is ours
and that mastered by our fears
we succumb to lethal powers,
yet this day we shall not yield,
for by grace we'll seek release
till the weeping reddened field
shall be stilled with heaven's peace.

125. God of Mercy and Compassion

God of mercy and compassion,
who counts our tears
and hears our sighs
and knows the secrets of our hearts,
we acknowledge that bitter memories
and hopes of revenge
often choke our best intentions.
Lost in the past,
we forget that it is a good and joyful thing,
always and everywhere to give thanks to you.
Release us from our violent dreams
and fill us with gracious visions
of the world that would come to be,
if we sang your song in this strange land
and embodied the love
that we know through Christ Jesus our Lord.

126. Lions and Oxen Will Feed in the Hay

Lions and oxen will feed in the hay,
leopards will join with the lambs as they play,
wolves will be pastured with cows in the glade—
blood will not darken the earth that God made.

Little child whose bed is straw,
take new lodgings in my heart.
Bring the dream Isaiah saw:
life redeemed from fang and claw.

Peace will pervade more than forest and field:
God will transfigure the violence concealed
deep in the heart and in systems of gain,
ripe for the judgment the Lord will ordain.

Little child whose bed is straw,
take new lodgings in my heart.
Bring the dream Isaiah saw:
justice purifying law.

Nature reordered to match God's intent,
nations obeying the call to repent,
all of creation completely restored,
filled with the knowledge and love of the Lord!

Little child whose bed is straw,
take new lodgings in my heart.
bring the dream Isaiah saw:
knowledge, wisdom, worship, awe.

127. God Made from One Blood All the Families of Earth

God made from one blood all the families of earth,
the circles of nurture that raised us from birth,
companions who join us to walk through each stage
of childhood and youth and adulthood and age.

We turn to you, God, with our thanks and our tears
for all of the families we've known through the years,
the intimate networks on whom we depend
of parent and partner and roommate and friend.

We learn through families how our closeness and trust
increase when our actions are loving and just
yet families have also distorted their roles,
mistreating their members and bruising their souls.

Give, Lord, each family lost in conflict and storm
a sense of your wisdom and grace that transform
sharp anger to insight which strengthens the heart
and makes clear the place where rebuilding can start.

Make wide that wisdom and that grace to include
the races and viewpoints our families exclude
till peace in each home bears and nurtures the bud
of peace shared by all you have made from one blood.

128. If Christ Is Charged with Madness

If Christ is charged with madness,
it's madness that's divine,
a visionary gladness
this world cannot confine,
the madness of conceiving
what no one else can see,
then acting and believing
so it will come to be.

Thus when Christ seized and plundered
the demons' dark domain,
his friends and foes both wondered
if he were not insane.
They charged his soul was riven,
his heart and mind possessed
by forces he had driven
from those who were distressed.

Christ spoke to all this ranting,
a vivid, lucid word
a parable supplanting
the charges he had heard.
"A house that is divided,
a kingdom, soul or land
with raging wars inside it
cannot survive and stand."

Despite his deft explaining,
Christ still appeared distraught
to guardians maintaining
accepted bounds of thought.
The force of faith in action
seems madness to each age
and often the reaction
is fear disguised as rage.

Yet earth needs heaven's madness
to seize with grace and bind
the guilt, the hurt, the sadness,
the fear and hate that blind.
Intrude, O Christ, impassioned
with madness that's divine
upon the world we've fashioned
and give it your design.

129. As Servants Working an Estate

As servants working an estate
whose owner is away,
and whose return they all await
though no one knows the day,
so none of us can name the hour,
the season or the year
when Christ with all of heaven's power
will suddenly appear.

Our task is not to calculate
what angels do not know,
but faithfully to watch and wait
and Christ's compassion show.
Not loading fragile human schemes
with hopes they cannot bear,
we trust the promise that redeems
the present from despair.

For Christ the Lord will surely come,
the king whom kings will fear,
and with God's perfect justice plumb
the justice we do here,
revealing that the present age
and every age that's past
are not the final moral gauge
that judges us at last.

So guide, Lord Christ, our every choice
that when our hearts shall hear
your step, your knock, your calling voice
we will not hide in fear,
but welcome you from realms above
to your estate below,
where justice, mercy, peace and love
abundantly will grow.

130. How Buoyant and Bold the Stride of Christ's Friends

How buoyant and bold the stride of Christ's friends
when swept by his words like high lifting winds
they set out to preach and to heal in the land
with nothing to take but a staff in their hand.

Not slowed by the bulk and drag of great loads,
to cities and towns, on pathways and roads,
they carried the glad urgent gospel of grace
that beat in their hearts and drummed in their pace.

Christ sent them in twos instead of alone
to tell the good news wherever unknown
and lift up each other when hurt and confused
because what they offered was mocked and refused.

Approaching a town or high city wall,
they wondered what soul awaited Christ's call
and who would react with disinterest or scorn
and how many others by doubt would be torn.

Lord, grant us a faith so brave and so bright
that we too shall dare to travel as light
as those who took nothing but what they would need
to bring peace and healing with grace and with speed.

131. Seek for the Kingdom with All of Your Powers

Seek for the kingdom with all of your powers!
Live by your faith, not the fear in your bone.
Think on the raven, consider the flowers:
all that is living is cherished and known.

More than the beauty that brightens the field,
more than the wings that are flashing in flight,
Jesus in dying and rising revealed
we are encompassed by love and by light.

Seek then the kingdom discerning its signs:
peace that defuses the weapons of death,
justice defeating oppression's designs,
healing that strengthens our pulse and our breath.

Seek for the kingdom with body and mind.
Seek it by action and strenuous thought.
Seek, and in seeking by grace you will find
wonders surpassing the wonders you sought.

132. From Pharaoh to King Cyrus

From Pharaoh to King Cyrus
to Alexander's reign
to Caesar's PAX ROMANA
there marched a haughty train
of potentates and despots
each acting as a god,
demanding praise and homage
from every land they trod.

Their palaces have crumbled,
their scepters, crowns and thrones,
and where their armies rumbled
the soil is chalk from bones.
Thus Pontius Pilate's vanished
who wielded Caesar's sword,
yet lives the one he banished:
our risen reigning Lord!

Let tyrants and their minions
who plot how they will bend
the world to be their servants
hear Christ who calls us "friend."
No threat from modern Caesars,
no order to obey
what contradicts the gospel
shall turn us from Christ's way.

Clear notes of liberation
are trilling in our hearts:
they are the pulse of conscience
our dauntless friend imparts,
the quickened beat for justice
that thickens timid blood,
supplying us with courage
to stem earth's violent flood.

Christ's high rhapsodic vision
of truth and love and peace
has loosened dreams and yearnings
that will not fade or cease.
We fear no earthly power
for we are claimed as friends
by that all-gracious ruler
whose kingdom never ends.

133. No Dusk, but Sudden Night

No dusk, but sudden night,
no time to stretch the day,
to talk in lingering light
and see you on your way.

I conjure up a kiss
and one long last embrace—
I dream the parting that we missed
and I wake by night to trace

your quick long stride
when you first took me for a climb
and you scrambled up the mountainside
while I stopped and took my time.

Then you came back for me,
and I knew you would be more than a friend
when you said, "Come and see
the view around the bend."

I pray you now have sped
up some great hidden height
to find there lies ahead
no dawn, but sudden light.

134. When There Is No Star to Guide You

When there is no star to guide you
and you cannot wait for day
and your ancient maps provide you
only hints to find the way,
keep within each other's calling,
mark each time you make a turn,
shout for help if you are falling,
tell each other all you learn.

Be alert to shifts in weather:
if it turns to cold and frost
huddle closely all together,
check if any have been lost.
Listen for a river flowing,
feel for damper, moving air,
trace from where the wind is blowing,
move on bravely but with care.

If you think you have discovered
with your lantern in the night
some clear path the dark has covered
let the others bring their light.
Test your single lone perception
in their gathered shining beams,
what you saw may be projection
fed by shadows, fears and dreams.

You may sometimes trip and stumble
on a hidden root or stone
but remember as you grumble
that you do not fall alone.
And in risking dark expanses
never marked on map or chart
you will find that faith advances
through the landscape of your heart.

Afterword

Although my hymns owe a great deal to the legacy of English and American congregational song, they also represent an effort to expand those traditions by challenging some commonly held assumptions about hymnody. I reject, for example, the sharp distinction that is often made between poems and hymns. Setting the two in opposition goes back, I believe, at least as far Matthew Arnold, and the contrast is maintained by some of the finest contemporary writers of hymns.

No less an artist than Fred Pratt Green introduces his recent work by observing: "The first time I saw myself described as a poet and hymn writer I felt uneasy. Although the two must be related, they make an odd pair."[1] In a similar fashion, Timothy Dudley-Smith says in a foreword to one of his collections, "I have written few lines intended as poetry rather than as hymns."[2]

Despite these claims, I believe the best of their work has an enduring appeal precisely because it *is* poetic. By poetic I mean verse that satisfies "hungers for emotional force, boldness, and grandeur that are always present in readers of poetry,"[3]—and, I would add, in those who gather to worship and sing hymns. It is regular churchgoers who have heightened my appreciation for these hungers. Whenever they learn that I teach preaching, they tell me: "I hope you are teaching your students to inspire people." This remark often leads to a conversation about their yearning to be lifted up by a vision of grace and beauty that can sustain their efforts for justice and kindness in the brutal workaday world. I believe that to draw a sharp distinction between hymns and poetry is to negate one of the major ways that the church can address this hunger of the human soul to be inspired. If we fail to maintain the poetic vitality of hymnody, we run the risk of becoming "hectoring and didactic and fierce, as the 18th century writers [of hymns], when not at the top of their inspiration, were liable to be."[4]

I place poetic hymnody in the context of the church's need for a wide range of congregational song, including the simplicity of folk lyrics and the rigor of "versified dogma, stating incontrovertible truths in square solid verse not intended to be judged as poetry."[5]   These, too, have their function in the liturgical life of the church. But neither simplicity or dogma alone can keep liturgical language vital. The poetic expressiveness of faith is also essential because "to lose the *vis poetica* is at the same time to lose the *vis religiosa*."[6]

It appears that the propensity to draw a sharp line between hymns and poems can be traced to certain understandings of poetry and the imagination that began to take root in the romantic period and that have grown stronger and more expansive through the modern era.   T. S. Eliot helps us understand this shift through his distinction between "classical" and "romantic" poets. By the former he means those who

> arrive at poetry through eloquence. . . . Wisdom has the primacy over inspiration . . . [and they] are more concerned with the world about them than with their own joys and sorrows, and concerned with their own feelings in their likeness to those of other men [and women] rather than in their particularity.[7]

Part of why contemporary hymnists may distinguish their work from poetry is that they have accepted the "romantic" definition of poetry which focuses on the "particularity" of the poetic voice rather than upon its communal dimension, what the poet has in "likeness" to the rest of humanity. It is this limited definition that seems to influence Fred Pratt Green when he writes: "The poet, as such, writes to please himself. His vision is personal and private. And he is rarely a conformist, a characteristic he shares with most other artists."[8]

This perspective is confirmed by some modern critics, such as Helen Vendler, who puts the matter as strongly as possible:

> The price paid for individuality of voice—the quality, after all, for which we remember poets—is absolute social

184

singularity. Each poet is a species to himself, a mutant in the human herd, speaking an idiolect he shares with no one."[9]

Some recent literary criticism, however, has challenged the overly privatized poetic voice. For example, Czeslaw Milosz, winner of the Nobel prize for literature, writes that

Twentieth-century poetry suffered "impoverishment and narrowing" because its interests became limited to "an aesthetic and nearly always individualistic order." In other words, it withdrew from the domain common to all people into the closed circle of subjectivism.[10]

Part of the role of a hymn writer is to step out of "the closed circle of subjectivism," to be in Eliot's term, a "classical" poet.

To put the matter another way, a hymn writer strives to find the balance between the community and the individual, between what Wendell Berry calls a "language so commonized by generality or jargon or slang that one's own mind and life virtually disappear into it," and "a language made so personal by contrivance, affectation, or slovenliness that one makes no sense."[11] To find the balance between these is to write as a classical poet, to create work that moves from a privatized imagination toward a public consciousness.

Thus the debate about the relationship of poetry and hymnody turns out to involve far more than a difference in literary judgments. It concerns how we will draw upon the visionary gifts of artists for the healing of communities as well as for the expression of personal experience and meaning. The disavowal of hymns as poetry is symptomatic of a deeper breakdown between religious faith and imagination in the white western world. There is a strong bias against imagination, and therefore against the poetic, in the history of Christianity.[12] To acknowledge the poetry of hymns and to write hymns in an intentionally poetic style is one way to overcome the historic breach between imagination and faith.

This does not mean all poets should write as classical poets. I am enriched by what Vendler calls the "idiolect" of many of our twentieth-century poets. But even if fed by these idiolects, hymn writers give witness to another style of expression that is just as poetic and demanding as the current literary fashion.

I believe the time is ripe for reclaiming through hymnody the classical, communal dimensions of poetry because both literary criticism and theology are developing a greater sense of how texts can be viewed "as symptoms of the larger super-text that is culture."[13] There is a growing consciousness of how all speech and writing, including poetry, is an extension of the web of language, value and meaning which interconnects us.

This awareness includes a heightened theological sensitivity to the tyrannies of language, the hierarchies of power which are reflected and reinforced by the way we talk about reality. Thus Marjorie Procter-Smith calls attention to the confining nature of our inherited liturgical language and the imagined world it expresses:

> About imagination, we say that our ability to imagine a future church in which women are not silent and marginal has been constricted. Our ability to imagine God as anything other than an old man, or to imagine our selves, women and men, as free and mutually empowering people, has been constricted. Our imaginations (and not just women's) have been colonized.[14]

To de-colonize the liturgical imagination of congregational song requires "a whole new poetry."[15] Developing a whole new poetry in hymnody is a complex process, especially if, like myself, one wants to work within and on behalf of the church. Tradition by its nature never changes instantly from one thing to the other. My solution has been to write hymns that employ the pleasures and conventions of rhyme, euphony, and strong regular meters. However, in doing so I have deliberately pulled and stretched the hymnic form to give new vitality to the poetic devices and to join in the process of de-colonizing the liturgical imagination which many other hymnists, theologians, and liturgists have begun.

"Startled by a Holy Humming" is an example of what I mean by stretching the hymnic form. Although it is written to a standard hymn meter, and printed that way in this collection, here is how I originally heard the opening lines in my head:

Startled
by a holy
humming,
drumming
in her heart and ear,
Mary
heard an angel
coming,
Gabriel
was drawing near.

It was the dropping trochaic beat that initiated the poem and propelled its creation. In Carol Doran's setting, a minor third on the key words, *startled*, *humming*, *drumming*, and *coming*, captures perfectly the sonic sense of this beat.[16]

"God Made from One Blood All the Families of Earth" is an example of what I mean by de-colonizing the liturgical imagination. In this case, the poetry replaces the image of the nuclear family that dominates many churches with a recognition of the wide variations in understandings of what constitutes a family:

We turn to you, God, with our thanks and our tears
for all of the families we've known through the years,
the intimate networks on whom we depend
of parent and partner and roommate and friend.

In content and style these hymns represent my small contribution to the great liberating movement of a more inclusive religious idiom which is being carried on by pastors, theologians, poets, liturgists, biblical interpreters, and thoughtful Christians around the world. I, as all the others, will only sometimes succeed and often falter, but the task is essential if we are to have a faith that does not in the name of God reinforce patterns of exclusion and domination.

I am also writing these hymns for evangelical reasons: to reach peripheral believers, those who encounter the holy through common experience but who feel awkward claiming that experience through traditional hymnic language because of its distance from contemporary idiom. I am striving for a language that maps the territory shared in common by the believer and those who hunger to name the larger dimensions of their experience but fear their aesthetic and intellectual integrity will be muffled by an overconstraining piety.

The great American modern poet Wallace Stevens, whose sensibilities have influenced my own consciousness even though I do not share his theological conclusions, once wrote:

The major poetic idea in the world is and always has been the idea of God. One of the visible movements of the modern imagination is the movement away from the idea of God. The poetry that created the idea of God will either adapt it to our different intelligence, or create a substitute for it, or make it unnecessary. . . .[17]

I have chosen the first of these options, adapting the idea of God to our different intelligence. To use a term from systematic theology, I am writing "apologetic" verse, interpreting faith to the culture. I aim to do this in poetry that fills the requirements of hymnody, including immediate accessibility of meaning, but poetry which at the same time draws the singer or reader to deeper considerations, worthy of attention beyond the brief span of singing the stanzas in a service.

The lyric poems and prayers interspersed throughout this collection extend the process of theological and spiritual meditation in a number of ways. The most obvious is that sometimes the lyric poem has given me a word-for-word line or a concept for a hymn. For example, the title and opening line of the hymn, "The Lick of the Tide, the Lunge of the Storm," was drawn directly from the lyric verse, "A New Line of Shore." Likewise, the idea of doubting Thomas reading Christ's palms as braille in "These Things Did Thomas Count as Real" came to me upon re-reading "I Walk the Farm I Never

Walked," a poem which I had written several years earlier for my wife and her mother, the two M. M.s in the poem's dedication.

But more important than these literal connections is the perceptual and spiritual process which the lyric poems make clear. One can trace in these pieces my sense of how the simplest objects—a lawn mower in "A Fixed Sum," a hammer in "Pounding a Nail in My Cellar Shop"—become bearers of grace. I build upon the sacramental overtones of common experience in these verses, and it is my listening to these overtones which has stirred me to the imagery and sound of the hymns.

All of the poetry and prayers in this book can, then, be understood as a small part of the enormous theological task of re-imaging the gospel. Or to use Wallace Stevens's terms, they are my attempt to "adapt" the idea of God "to our different intelligence":

> We work and pray to gain
> a vision of the range
> that rises in the mind
> as science, thought and culture change
> how faith will be defined.

The endeavor to transform religious consciousness, to purify it of oppressive and authoritarian elements, will never be won purely by an appeal to reason. It also requires that we move the heart with language that meets the "hungers for emotional force, boldness, and grandeur."[18] A church that is afraid to reach for such expression, even if it does not always attain the goal, will lose contact with the "Wind who makes all winds that blow." But a church that risks poetic idioms filled with the stress and strain of thinking faith may feel anew the power of God:

> The highest peaks are found
> where plates of bedrock shift.
> Disturbance of the solid ground

is God's creative gift,
who still is sculpting earth
and uses that same art
around the world to bring to birth
new landscapes in the heart.

Notes

1. Fred Pratt Green, *Later Hymns and Ballads and Fifty Poems* (Carol Stream, Ill.: Hope Publishing Company, 1989), p. xiii.

2. Timothy Dudley-Smith, *Lift Every Heart: Collected Hymns, 1961–1983 and Some Early Poems* (Carol Stream, Ill.: Hope Publishing Company, 1984), p. 13.

3. The words were originally written to explain the wide appeal of Dylan Thomas's poetry. David Perkins, *A History of Modern Poetry, Modernism and After* (Cambridge, Mass.: The Belknap Press of Harvard University Press, 1987), p. 177.

4. Erik Routley, *Christian Hymns Observed: When in Our Music God Is Glorified* (Princeton, N.J.: Prestige Publications, 1982).

5. Jaroslav J. Vajda, *Now the Joyful Celebration: Hymns, Carols, and Songs* (St. Louis: Morning Star Music Publishers, 1987), p. 188. In describing certain chorales that have this ponderous quality, Vajda observes that the result is "a boring exercise for many worshipers, especially those for whom the chorale is strange."

6. Wilbur Marshall Urban, *Language and Reality* (London: George Allen & Unwin, 1939), p. 575 as quoted in Nathan A. Scott, Jr., *The Poetics of Belief, Studies in Coleridge, Arnold, Pater, Santayana, Stevens, and Heidegger* (Chapel Hill: The University of North Carolina Press, 1985), p. 47.

7. T. S. Eliot, ed., *A Choice of Kipling's Verse Made by T. S. Eliot with an Essay on Rudyard Kipling* (New York: Charles Scribner's Sons, 1943), p. 26.

8. Green, *Later Hymns*, p. xv.

9. Helen Vendler, *New York Times Book Review*, 14 Oct. 1984, p. 41.

10. Czeslaw Milosz, *The Witness of Poetry* (Cambridge, Mass.: Harvard University Press, 1983), p. 26. In the quotations within the quotation he is drawing on the work of a distant relative of his, Oscar Milosz.

11. Wendell Berry, *Standing by Words* (San Francisco: North Point Press, 1983), p. 207.

12. For a brief historic account of the split between Christian faith and imagination see my book, *Imagining a Sermon* (Nashville, Tenn.: Abingdon, 1990), ch. 6.

13. Robert Scholes, *Protocols of Reading* (New Haven, Conn.: Yale University Press, 1989), p. 31.

14. Marjorie Procter-Smith, *In Her Own Rite: Constructing Feminist Liturgical Tradition* (Nashville, Tenn.: Abingdon Press, 1990), p. 19.

15. Ibid., p. 66. Here Proctor-Smith is drawing upon the poetry of Adrienne Rich.

16. Carol Doran and Thomas H. Troeger, *New Hymns for the Lectionary: To Glorify the Maker's Name* (New York: Oxford University Press, 1986), no. 19.

17. Quoted in Milton J. Bates, *Wallace Stevens: A Mythology of Self* (Berkeley: University of California Press, 1985), p. 212.

18. See n. 3.

Notes on Meter, Scriptural References, and Occasion

Numbers refer to the number of the text, not the page number.

1. The Moon with Borrowed Light

   Meter: S. M. D. (6–6–8–6 D)
   Scripture: John 1:6–9, 19–28
   Occasion: Year B, Advent 3.

2. Swiftly Pass the Clouds of Glory

   Meter: 8–7–8–7 D
   Scripture: Mark 9:2–13 and parallels
   Occasion: The feast of the Transfiguration; the last
                   Sunday after Epiphany.

3. Density of Light

   Meter: Irregular
   Scripture: Mark 9:2–13 and parallels
   Occasion: Written at the request of the composer
                   John Kuzma. For an anthem on the
                   Transfiguration he wanted some free
                   verses that a narrator could speak,
                   interspersing them between the stanzas of
                   hymn 2, "Swiftly Pass the Clouds of Glory."

4. Let the Truth Shine in Our Speaking

   Meter: 8–7–8–7 D
   Scripture: Ephesians 4:25–5:2
   Occasion: Year B, Pentecost 12.

5. Listen to the Cloud that Brightens

Meter: 8-7-8-7 D
Scripture: Hebrews 12:1-2
Occasion: All Saints. Written especially for the retirement of Bishop Robert Spears.

6. Writing at Dusk

Meter: Irregular
Scripture: None
Occasion: Written for the poet S. Panaretos.

7. Direct Us, Lord, through Darkness

Meter: 7-6-7-6 D
Scripture: Various passages about stars and creation
Occasion: Written upon seeing planetary photographs from a space probe.

8. The Hidden Stream that Feeds

Meter: S.M. (6-6-8-6) with refrain of 8-8
Scripture: John 4:7-15
Occasion: Written as the first commission for the Rev. Marilyle Sweet Page.

9. Water Moving through Stone

Meter: Irregular
Scripture: Various passages about the Spirit
Occasion: Written to help a friend pray for the Spirit.

10. The First Day of Creation

Meter: 7-6-7-6 D
Scripture: Genesis 1:1ff. and II Corinthians 5:17
Occasion: Year B, Pentecost 4.

11. God Marked a Line and Told the Sea

Meter: L. M. (8-8-8-8)
Scripture: Job 38:8-11
Occasion: Written to counter a surfeit of
              antinomian sermons.

12. A New Line of Shore

Meter: Irregular
Scripture: Various passages about covenant
Occasion: The remembrance of restored friendships
              and marriages.

13. The Lick of the Tide, the Lunge of the Storm

Meter: 10-10-11-11
Scripture: Romans 8:31-39
Occasion: Funerals, memorial services.

14. The Sails Were Spilling Wind

Meter: 6-6-6-6-8-8
Scripture: Mark 4:35-41
Occasion: Year B, Pentecost 5.

15. On the Sand, in the Sun

Meter: Irregular
Scripture: None
Occasion: Aria for an opera in progress.

16. Praise to the Spinner Who Twisted and Twirled

Meter: 10-11-11-12
Scripture: Psalm 104:1-2
Occasion: The ordination of Leona Irsch as a priest.

17. Who Commands Vast Worlds in Motion?

Meter: Follows a meter from Tanzanian music
Scripture: Various creation and redemption passages
Occasion This is a translation/paraphrase of Pote Atawala Nan, a hymn from Tanzania. It was requested by Howard S. Olson, who provided a literal translation which has been substantially altered in order to keep the rhythm and rhyme scheme of the original.

18. Source and Sovereign, Rock and Cloud

Meter: 7-7-7-7 with refrain of 7-7-7-7
Scripture: Various passages supplied the images of God
Occasion: A request from the United Methodist Church for a hymn on the wide ranging imagery for God that is found in the Bible. The refrain has been modified from the way it first appeared in *The United Methodist Hymnal*, 1989.

19. Source and Sovereign of All Creation

Meter: Irregular
Scripture: Romans 8:38-39
Occasion: A litany to go with the hymns "Source and Sovereign" and "The Lick of the Tide."

20. The Sheep Stood Stunned in Sudden Light

Meter: L. M. (8-8-8-8)
Scripture: Luke 2:1-21
Occasion: Christmas. The poem reverses the image of the receding sea of faith in Matthew Arnold's "Dover Beach."

21.   Wild the Man and Wild the Place

   Meter: 7-7-7-7
   Scripture: Mark 1:1-8
   Occasion: Year B, Advent 2; Nativity of St. John the
                 Baptist.

22.   What King Would Wade through Murky Streams

   Meter: C. M. (8-6-8-6) with refrain
   Scripture: Mark 1:9-11 and parallels
   Occasion: For baptisms and the remembrance of
                 baptisms; Baptism of Our Lord (Epiphany
                 1).

23.   O Praise the Gracious Power

   Meter: S. M. (6-6-8-6) with refrain
   Scripture: Ephesians 2:11-22
   Occasion: Written for the ordination of Judith Ray.
                 Also the feast of the Holy Cross.

24.   O Gracious Power

   Meter: Irregular
   Scripture: Ephesians 2:11-22
   Occasion: Written as a prayer for a service using "O
                 Praise the Gracious Power."

25.   Praise the Source of Faith and Learning

   Meter: 8-7-8-7 D
   Scripture: Psalm 139:6
   Occasion: Commissioned by Duke University to
                 honor Waldo Beach. The hymn is based
                 on the school motto, "Faith and Learning."

26. First the Wind upon the Water

Meter: 8-7-8-7 plus 8-8-7-7-9-6-8-7
Scripture: Genesis 1:1ff.
Occasion: Easter Vigil; Earth Day.

27. The Bush in Flame but Not Consumed

Meter: C. M. D. (8-6-8-6 D)
Scripture: Exodus 3:1-6
Occasion: Written for the ordination of Julie
              Fewster.

28. Though Every Sun Shall Spend Its Fire

Meter: L. M. (8-8-8-8)
Scripture: Luke 2:22-40
Occasion: Christmas 1; The Presentation of Our
              Lord.

29. Wind Who Makes All Winds that Blow

Meter: 7-7-7-7 D
Scripture: Acts 2:1-13
Occasion: Pentecost. First written for Father
              Sebastian Falcone of St. Bernard's
              Institute, Rochester, New York.

30. As Trees that Withstand the Wind's Shaking

Meter: Written to fit the Celtic Alleluia
Scripture: Psalm 1 and other passages about trees
Occasion: Written for a ritual dedicating the planting of
              a tree in memory of Gene Bartlett, former
              president of Colgate Rochester Divinity
              School.

31. A Single Leaf

    Meter: Irregular
    Scripture: Echoes of various passages about the cross
    Occasion: Written for Teresa Nolette, a friend who
                 admired the bright red, hand–like shape of
                 the leaves of the Japanese maple in my
                 backyard.

32. We Travel toward a Land Unknown

    Meter: 8-6-10-8-8-8-10-7
    Scripture: Genesis 12:1-3
    Occasion: Written for church anniversaries.

33. Go Forth with the Blessing of God

    Meter: Irregular
    Scripture: Genesis 12:1-3
    Occasion: Written as a benediction to follow "We
                 Travel toward a Land Unknown."

34. Why Stare at Heaven's Distant Blue

    Meter: 8-8-8-8-8-8
    Scripture: Acts 1:1-14
    Occasion: Ascension.

35. Far Easier to Melt the Gold

    Meter: C. M. (8-6-8-6)
    Scripture: Exodus 20:4-6
    Occasion: Composed to accompany an exercise on
                 images of God.

36. God, You Move among Us with Grace

Meter: Irregular
Scripture: John 3:7
Occasion: A prayer of confession to use with "Far Easier to Melt the Gold" or "Suddenly God's Sovereign Wind."

37. Suddenly God's Sovereign Wind

Meter: 7-7-7 D
Scripture: John 3:1–8
Occasion: Year B, Trinity.

38. Eagles' Spiralings Comply

Meter: 7-7-7-7-7-7-7 with refrain
Scripture: No one passage, but the theme of discipline
Occasion: Written upon hearing too many wandering sermons, many of which used the image of birds in flight.

39. The Song and Prayer of Birds

Meter: 6-6-6-6
Scripture: Romans 8:26
Occasion: A service explaining the ministry of music as a form of prayer.

40. Glory to God Is the Song of the Stars

Meter: 10-10-10 D with refrain
Scripture: Psalm 19, John 15:1ff.
Occasion: For the dedication of an organ. The biblical passages were chosen by those who commissioned the hymn.

41.   With Pipes of Tin and Wood Make Known

Meter: C. M. D. (8–6–8–6 D)
Scripture: Psalm 150 and other passages
Occasion: The dedication of a new pipe organ.

42.   Make Our Church One Joyful Choir

Meter: 7–7–7–7 with refrain
Scripture: Mark 8:34
Occasion: The refurbishing of a chancel, organ, and
                cross on a steeple.

43.   We Need Each Other's Voice to Sing

Meter: C. M. D. (8–6–8–6 D) with refrain
Scripture: Psalm 150 and other passages
Occasion: The wedding of two church musicians.

44.   Come Singing, Come Singing

Meter: Follows a meter from Tanzanian music
Scripture: Various passages about redemption and
                music
Occasion: This is a translation/paraphrase of "Sifuni,
                Sifuni," a hymn from Tanzania. It was
                requested by Howard S. Olson, who
                provided a literal translation which has
                been substantially altered in order to keep
                the rhythm and rhyme scheme of the
                original.

45.   Pastor, Lead Our Circle Dance

   Meter: 7–7–7–7 D
   Scripture: 2 Samuel 6:14
   Occasion: The installation, ordination or consecration
                 of a church leader. For *Pastor* substitute:
                 Elder, Deacon, Teacher, Bishop, etc.

46.   Make Your Prayer and Music One

   Meter: 7–7–7–7 with Alleluias
   Scripture: Acts 16:25ff.
   Occasion: Celebration of the ministries of music.

47.   The Love that Lifted Lyric Praise

   Meter: L. M. D. (8–8–8–8 D)
   Scripture: 2 Samuel 23:1–7
   Occasion: A sermon based on the life of King David.

48.   Too Splendid for Speech but Ripe for a Song

   Meter: 10–10–11–11
   Scripture: Psalm 98
   Occasion: Celebration of the ministries of music.

49.   With Glad, Exuberant Carolings

   Meter: 8–6–8–6–8–6
   Scripture: Ephesians 5:15–20
   Occasion: A hymn of joyful adoration.

50.   Startled by a Holy Humming

   Meter: 8–7–8–7 D
   Scripture: Luke 1:26–38
   Occasion: The Annunciation; sermons about Mary;
                 the Commemoration of Mary.

51. Sing with Gabriel the Greeting

Meter: 8-7-8-7 D with refrain
Scripture: Luke 1:26-38
Occasion: The Annunciation; sermons about Mary;
                    the Commemoration of Mary.

52. God of Gabriel

Meter: Irregular
Scripture: Luke 1:26-38
Occasion: The Annunciation; the Commemoration of
                    Mary; written to be used with "Startled by
                    a Holy Humming" and "Sing with Gabriel
                    the Greeting."

53. In the Babble of a Baby

Meter: 8-7-6-7
Scripture: Mark 14:36, Romans 8:15, 16
Occasion: Sermons on prayer and images of God.

54. Blessed Be You, O God

Meter: Irregular
Scripture: Psalm 8
Occasion: To be used with any of the hymns listed
                    under "music" in the index according to
                    theme and image.

55. May the God Whose Music Sounded

Meter: Irregular
Scripture: None in particular
Occasion: The departure of a church musician.

56. Gangling Desert Birds Will Sing

Meter: 7-7-7-7 D
Scripture: Isaiah 43:16-25
Occasion: Sermons on new life, new creation.

57. A Spendthrift Lover Is the Lord

Meter: C. M. D. (8-6-8-6 D)
Scripture: John 3:14-21
Occasion: Weddings; sermons on love.

58. Instead of a King

Meter: 5-5-6-5-6-7-6-6
Scripture: Isaiah 49:14-18
Occasion: Sermons dealing with the images of God.

59. Holy and Good Is the Gift of Desire

Meter: 6-5-6-5-5-5-6-5 with refrain
Scripture: Genesis 2:21-25
Occasion: Sermons addressing sexual abuse.

60. Far More than Passion's Passing Flame

Meter: C. M. (8-6-8-6)
Scripture: Mark 10:2-16
Occasion: Weddings, anniversaries.

61. Unbidden Came God's Love

Meter: 6-6-6-6
Scripture: John 1:14
Occasion: Weddings, anniversaries. First written as a
               poem for my wife.

62. Twenty-five Years

Meter: Irregular
Scripture: None
Occasion: Silver wedding anniversary.

63. On Bringing a Friend Purple Tulips

Meter: Irregular
Scripture: None
Occasion: Sermons on friendship and power
relationships.

64. A Single Unmatched Stone

Meter: 6–6–6–6–8–8
Scripture: Acts 4:5–12
Occasion: Year B, Easter 4.

65. The Word of God Was from the Start

Meter: L. M. (8–8–8–8)
Scripture: John 1:1–14
Occasion: Sermons on the incarnation.

66. The Hands that First Held Mary's Child

Meter: C. M. D. (8–6–8–6 D)
Scripture: Matthew 1:18–25
Occasion: Christmas; St. Joseph.

67. Our Savior's Infant Cries Were Heard

Meter: C. M. (8–6–8–6)
Scripture: Matthew 2:13–15
Occasion: Holy Innocents; sermons about the care of
children; the Holy Family.

68.   A Star Not Mapped on Human Charts

Meter: C. M. D. (8–6–8–6 D)
Scripture: Matthew 2:1–12
Occasion: Epiphany.

69.   Neither Desert Wind Nor Sun

Meter: 7–7–7–7 D
Scripture: Mark 1:12–15
Occasion: Year B, Lent 1.

70.   To Those Who Knotted Nets of Twine

Meter: C. M. (8–6–8–6)
Scripture: Mark 1:14–20
Occasion: Sermons on call and discipleship; Apostles'
                days (Andrew, Peter, James, John).

71.   The Leper's Soul Was No Less Scarred

Meter: C. M. (8–6–8–6)
Scripture: Mark 1:40–45
Occasion: Sermons on the role of acceptance in
                healing.

72.   We Have the Strength to Lift and Bear

Meter: C. M. D. (8–6–8–6 D)
Scripture: Mark 2:1–12
Occasion: Sermons on healing and forgiveness.

73.   Soundless Were the Tossing Trees

Meter: 7–7–7–7 D
Scripture: Mark 7:31–37
Occasion: Sermons on healing and hearing.

74. Ballad of the Woman Bent Double

    Meter: 10–10–10–10
    Scripture: Luke 13:10–17
    Occasion: Sermons on liberation and healing.

75. Far From the Markets of Rich Meat and Wine

    Meter: 10–10–10–10
    Scripture: John 6:1–15
    Occasion: Sermons on Holy Communion; St. Philip; St. Andrew.

76. What Fabled Names from Judah's Past

    Meter: C. M. with refrain (8–6–8–6 8–8)
    Scripture: Mark 8:27–35
    Occasion: Sermons on the nature of the Christ; Confession of St. Peter.

77. A Cheering, Chanting, Dizzy Crowd

    Meter: C. M. (8–6–8–6)
    Scripture: Mark 11:1–11 and parallels
    Occasion: Palm Sunday.

78. Kneeling in the Garden Grass

    Meter: 7–7–7–7 with refrain of 7
    Scripture: The passion accounts of the gospels
    Occasion: Stations of the Cross. This sequence of stanzas matches the revised stations that the Vatican has observed in recent years. For the traditional sequence see number 79, "While the Court and Priests Conspire."

79.   While the Court and Priests Conspire

   Meter: 7-7-7-7 with refrain of 7
   Scripture: The passion accounts in the gospels
   Occasion: Stations of the Cross. This sequence of
                 stanzas matches the traditional sequence.
                 For the newer sequence see the
                 immediately preceding poem.

80.   Pounding a Nail in My Cellar Shop

   Meter: Irregular
   Scripture: No one particular passage
   Occasion: Celebration of a retired minister's life's
                 work.

81.   Crucified Savior

   Meter: Irregular
   Scripture: Psalm 139:7-12 and the passion narratives
   Occasion: For use with services in Holy Week and with
                 hymn 2, "Swiftly Pass the Clouds of Glory."

82.   No Iron Spike, No Granite Weight

   Meter: L. M. (8-8-8-8)
   Scripture: Mark 16:1-8
   Occasion: Easter, funerals, memorial services.

83.   Set Free, Set Free by God's Grace

   Meter: Follows a meter from Tanzanian music
   Scripture: Various redemption passages
   Occasion: This is a translation/paraphrase of "Kwa
                 Neema Na Pendo," a hymn from Tanzania.
                 It was requested by Howard S. Olson, who
                 provided a literal translation which has
                 been substantially altered in order to keep

the rhythm and rhyme scheme of the
original.

84.   Our Shepherd Is the Lamb

Meter: S. M. (6–6–8–6) with a refrain in S. M.
Scripture: Revelation 5:12
Occasion: Celebration of the eucharist. Originally
written for the installation of the Rev.
Marilyle Sweet Page as rector of the
Church of the Atonement.

85.   How Unlike All Earthly Glory

Meter: 8–7–8–7 D
Scripture: Revelation 5:12
Occasion: Celebration of the eucharist.

86.   Crown as Your King the King Who Came Crownless

Meter: 10–10–11–7 with refrain 7–7–7–8
Scripture: John 18:33–19:5
Occasion: Christ the King; Holy Cross.

87.   Through Our Fragmentary Prayers

Meter: 7–7–7–7
Scripture: Romans 8:26
Occasion: Sermons on prayer and the Spirit.

88.   The Branch that Bends with Clustered Fruit

Meter: C. M. (8–6–8–6)
Scripture: John 15:1–8
Occasion: Sermons on renewal.

89. Before the Fruit Is Ripened by the Sun

Meter: 10–10–10–10
Scripture: 12:20–33
Occasion: Easter, funerals, memorial services.

90. Let All Who Pray the Prayer Christ Taught

Meter: 8–6–8–6
Scripture: Matthew 6:9ff. and parallels
Occasion: To be sung before the Lord's Prayer.

91. Creator of All that Is

Meter: Irregular
Scripture: Genesis 1:26–27
Occasion: Prayer of confession.

92. Seek Not in Distant, Ancient Hills

Meter: C. M. (8–6–8–6)
Scripture: John 4:19–26
Occasion: Sermons on prayer and the inward journey.

93. As a Chalice Cast of Gold

Meter: 7–7–7 D
Scripture: Mark 7:14–15
Occasion: Sermons on purity of heart.

94. Searcher of Human Hearts

Meter: Irregular
Scripture: Various passages
Occasion: To be used with hymn 93, "As a Chalice."
               All Saints.

95. Forever in the Heart There Springs

Meter: L. M. D. (8-8-8-8 D)
Scripture: John 6:24-35
Occasion: Sermons on the eucharist.

96. If All You Want, Lord, Is My Heart

Meter: C. M. (8-6-8-6)
Scripture: Matthew 22:36ff. and parallels
Occasion: Sermons on discipleship and call.

97. Heart, Hold Fast

Meter: 3-3 with refrain of 6-4-3-1
Scripture: Revelation 2:13
Occasion: Service of rededication.

98. On a Visit South in January

Meter: Irregular
Scripture: Psalm 90:5-6
Occasion: Sermons on the place of death in life.

99. Unless This Day Be Holy

Meter: 7-6-7-6 D
Scripture: Deuteronomy 5:12-15
Occasion: Opening of a service of worship.

100. Beyond the Press and Pull of Crowds

Meter: C. M. (8-6-8-6)
Scripture: Mark 1:35
Occasion: Sermons on prayer and renewal.

101.   When Heaven's Voice Was Still

Meter: S. M. (6-6-8-6)
Scripture: 1 Samuel 3:1-10
Occasion: Sermons on prayer and the silence of God.

102.   Before the Temple's Great Stone Sill

Meter: C. M. (8-6-8-6)
Scripture: 2 Samuel 7:1-17
Occasion: Dedication of a new building of worship.

103.   All that Rises toward the Sky

Meter: 7-7-7-7 with refrain of 7-7
Scripture: Psalm 141:2
Occasion: Incensation of the altar.

104.   The Scantest Touch of Grace Can Heal

Meter: C. M. (8-6-8-6)
Scripture: Mark 5:21-43
Occasion: Sermons on grace and healing.

105.   A Fixed Sum

Meter: Irregular
Scripture: Various passages about grace
Occasion: Sermons on grace in common life.

106.   Silence! Frenzied, Unclean Spirit

Meter: 8-7-8-7 D
Scripture: Mark 1:21-28
Occasion: Services of healing, preaching on demons.

107. Wherever There Are Tyrant Voices

Meter: Irregular
Scripture: Mark 1:21–28 and other demon stories
Occasion: Written to be used with hymn 106,
              "Silence! Frenzied, Unclean Spirit."

108. Ask, Seek, Knock

Meter: 3-7-7-7-3-7 with a refrain 3-7-7
Scripture: Matthew 7:7
Occasion: Sermons on prayer and journey.

109. O Gracious Christ

Meter: Irregular
Scripture: Revelation 3:20
Occasion: Sermons on call and communion with
              Christ.

110. Where Mountains Lift the Eye

Meter: S. M. D. (6–6–8–6 D) with refrain
Scripture: Psalm 121:2
Occasion: Originally written for the centennial
              celebration of the Iliff School of Theology.
              Appropriate for sermons and services
              expanding our understanding of faith
              beyond narrow bounds.

111. God Folds the Mountains Out of Rock

Meter: L. M. D. (8–8–8–8 D)
Scripture: Job 28
Occasion: Sermons on ecology and peace.

112. The Least in God's Kingdom Is Greater than John

Meter: 11–11–11–11
Scripture: Matthew 11:11
Occasion: Sermons on the reign of God; John the Baptist.

113. The Christians Traveled Caesar's Roads

Meter: C. M. D. (8–6–8–6 D)
Scripture: Passages from Acts
Occasion: Commissioned for a historical celebration of the American Baptist Churches in New England.

114. The Faith We Sing Was Sown

Meter: 6–7–6–7–6–6–6–6
Scripture: Isaiah 61:1–2
Occasion: Originally commissioned for the jubilee of a diocese in Illinois. The hymn is appropriate for a church's anniversary celebrations.

115. Our Founders Cleared an Open Field

Meter: C. M. D. (8–6–8–6 D) with refrain
Scripture: Psalm 24:1–2
Occasion: The bicentennial of three churches in central New York State founded by Jonathan Edwards the younger. The hymn is appropriate for a church's anniversary celebrations.

116. The Cross on the Hill Is the Measuring Rod

Meter: 11-6-6-5-7-11, or by combining lines 2
              and 3
              and lines 4 and 5-11-12-12-11
Scripture: 1 Corinthians 1:18-25
Occasion: Holy Cross; sermons on the cross and the
              value systems of this world.

117. The Beauty of the Sound of the Bells

Meter: Irregular
Scripture: None in particular
Occasion: Sermons on the entangled history of the
              church.

118. The Rocks Would Shout if We Kept Still

Meter: C. M. (8-6-8-6) with refrain
Scripture: Luke 19:39-40
Occasion: Commissioned by the Academy of
              Homiletics for its twenty-fifth anniversary.
              Appropriate for celebrations of preaching
              and Palm Sunday.

119. These Things Did Thomas Count as Real

Meter: L. M. (8-8-8-8)
Scripture: John 20:19-31
Occasion: Easter; St. Thomas.

120. I Walk the Farm I Never Walked

Meter: Irregular
Scripture: None in particular
Occasion: Sermons trying to understand our
              relationship to the past.

215

121. Risen Christ, May Death Be Swift

Meter: 7-7-5-5-5
Scripture: 1 Corinthians 15:51-57
Occasion Written for a friend in the final stages of dying.

122. How Long, O Lord, How Long?

Meter: S. M. (6-6-8-6)
Scripture: Psalm 13
Occasion: For times of grief.

123. View the Present through the Promise

Meter: 8-5-8-5-8-8-8-5
Scripture: Various lections for Advent
Occasion: Advent or church anniversaries.

124. Fierce the Force that Curled Cain's Fist

Meter: 7-7-7-7 D
Scripture: Genesis 4:1-16
Occasion: Sermons on violence and peace.

125. God of Mercy and Compassion

Meter: Irregular
Scripture: Psalm 137
Occasion: Prayer of confession. Can be used with hymn 124, "Fierce the Force that Curled Cain's Fist."

126. Lions and Oxen Will Feed in the Hay

Meter: 10-10-10-10-7-7-7-7
Scripture: Isaiah 11:6-9
Occasion: Sermons on peace and Advent.

127. God Made from One Blood All the Families of Earth

Meter: 11-11-11-11
Scripture: Acts 17:26
Occasion: Sermons on families, peace and justice.

128. If Christ Is Charged with Madness

Meter: 7-6-7-6 D
Scripture: Mark 3:20-35
Occasion: Sermons explaining the gospel's conflict with the values of the world.

129. As Servants Working an Estate

Meter: C. M. D. (8-6-8-6 D)
Scripture: Mark 13:32-37
Occasion: Advent.

130. How Buoyant and Bold the Stride of Christ's Friends

Meter: 10-10-11-11
Scripture: Mark 6:7-13
Occasion: Sermons on evangelism and journey; feasts of Apostles and Evangelists.

131. Seek for the Kingdom with All of Your Powers

Meter: 10-10-10-10
Scripture: Matthew 6:25-33
Occasion: Sermons on the Sermon on the Mount.

132.	From Pharaoh to King Cyrus

Meter:	7–6–7–6 D
Scripture:	John 15:14–15
Occasion:	Sermons on the conflict between the gospel and the world.

133.	No Dusk, but Sudden Night

Meter:	Irregular
Scripture:	Revelation 22:5
Occasion:	Written for a friend whose husband suddenly died while traveling.

134.	When There Is No Star to Guide You

Meter:	8–7–8–7 D
Scripture:	Psalm 139:11–12
Occasion:	Written for a group requesting a post–modern hymn.

Metrical Index

221

Index by Theme and Image

233

Nativity of St. John the Baptist

Night

Ordination

Palm Sunday

Peace

Index by Scripture References

Index by First Line and Title

Most, but not all, titles are the first line.